Table of Contents

List of Figures

List of Tables

iv

STRENGTHENING U.S. CYBER SECURITY WITH THE VULNERABILITY MARKET

1. INTRODUCTION

In order to save money, increase automation, and facilitate information sharing between U.S agencies, the Department of Defense is acquiring new information systems at an increased rate[1]. These new information systems are more complex, interconnected, and interdependent than their predecessors in the DoD inventory. With these new capabilities comes a negative externality[2]; the more complex a system is, the more difficult it is to secure. Faced with this reality, the U.S. government is making a significant investment in cyber security. In the years between 2004 and 2009, the annual federal cyber security investment grew from $4.2 billion to $7.3 billion (a 73% increase). This amplified investment in cyber security focuses on establishing a frontline defense to prevent intrusions, integrating intelligence into cyber security, and shaping the future environment by enhancing research, development, and education. One gaping hole in this strategy is a focus on acquiring systems that are secure by design. This paper is a product of that gap and investigates whether the integration of a vulnerability market will increase overall DoD cyber security and lower the total cost of ownership for the systems it acquires.

---

[1] For this paper, the term Information System (IS) is used to describe a combination of computer hardware and computer software, data, and/or telecommunications that performs specified functions.
[2] A negative externality is a cost incurred by a party that is neither the buyer nor seller. An example of a negative externality is pollution.

1.1 Problem Statement

According to recent statistics from the Defense Acquisition University, approximately 60-70% of total life-cycle costs for a system occur in the operations and maintenance phase. The potential cost for patching software vulnerabilities in this phase increases as military systems become more complex and dependent on software. In order to limit the fiscal and physical impact of patching software vulnerabilities after a system has fielded, the DoD acquisition framework needs to implement a process that discovers, fixes, and deploys patches to software vulnerabilities as early as possible in the developmental phases of the acquisition lifecycle. This process, coupled with the already established defense-in-depth strategy, will ensure DoD information systems are maintainable, meet mission requirements, and remain secure against future advanced persistent threats.[3]

1.2 Research Question

The main objective of this research is to develop a quantitative model using a legitimate vulnerability market (VM) focused on identifying and avoiding software vulnerabilities as early as possible in the acquisition phases prior to production and deployment (Milestone C). The main research question this paper will seek to answer is:

In which way can a legitimate vulnerability market be used to reduce an information system's total cost of ownership while still maintaining Information Assurance and Mission Assurance controls prior to system deployment?

To reach the objective of establishing such a process, the following investigative questions need to be answered:

---

[3] An advanced persistent threat (APT) is an adversary with the capability and intent to persistently target an entity. APTs are traditionally organized groups or nation-states.

- What is "security" and can total "security" ever be achieved?
- How can the government hold IT vendors accountable for system security?
- What are the DoD's Information Assurance and Mission Assurance controls for IT systems?
- What is the current DoD Test and Evaluation process for IT acquisition?
- How is an exploited system's vulnerability impact quantified in private industry?
- What are the limitations of the methods currently used to ensure information assurance (IA) compliance in DoD systems?
- What is a vulnerability market (VM) and how is it applied in private industry?
- In order to reduce the total cost of ownership, what elements of "cost" must be considered?

1.3 Research Scope

The scope of this research project focuses on developing a vulnerability market model for the DoD acquisition process. Although the impact of an information system security incident includes much more than money, this research concentrates on the probabilistic cost of not fixing a software vulnerability and whether overall lifetime costs may be reduced using a vulnerability market. The model will seek to prove that the current cost assumed by DoD ($L_{no\ market}$) is greater than the cost of implementing a vulnerability market (L_{market}). P is the probability of attack against a particular vulnerability, AV is the value of the information secured by the system, EF is the system's exposure factor, and $Cost_{market}$ is the price to host a vulnerability market.

$$L_{no\ market} > L_{market}$$

$$L_{no\ market} = P_{attack}[(AV) \times (EF)]$$

$$L_{market} = P'_{attack}[(AV) \times (EF)] + Cost_{market}$$

This paper acknowledges that cost is multi-dimensional (e.g. integration, development, lost productivity) and that comparison to a security incident in private industry will be problematic. By restricting "cost" to a probabilistic outcome, this research project will formulate a legitimate vulnerability market model for use by the DoD. The objective of this VM model will be to significantly decrease total costs of software ownership by identifying system vulnerabilities early in the development and testing phases of the DoD acquisition cycle.

1.4 Research Methodology

The research project contains two main sections used to complete the project (see Figure 1.1). The first section explores the current practices by industry to discover and report system vulnerabilities. This section will also address the defense-in-depth and DIACAP strategies which form the backbone of the DoD information assurance policy. This section will include a detailed analysis of DoD information security/assurance controls as well as the common criteria of evaluated assurance levels outlined in DoDI 8500.1.

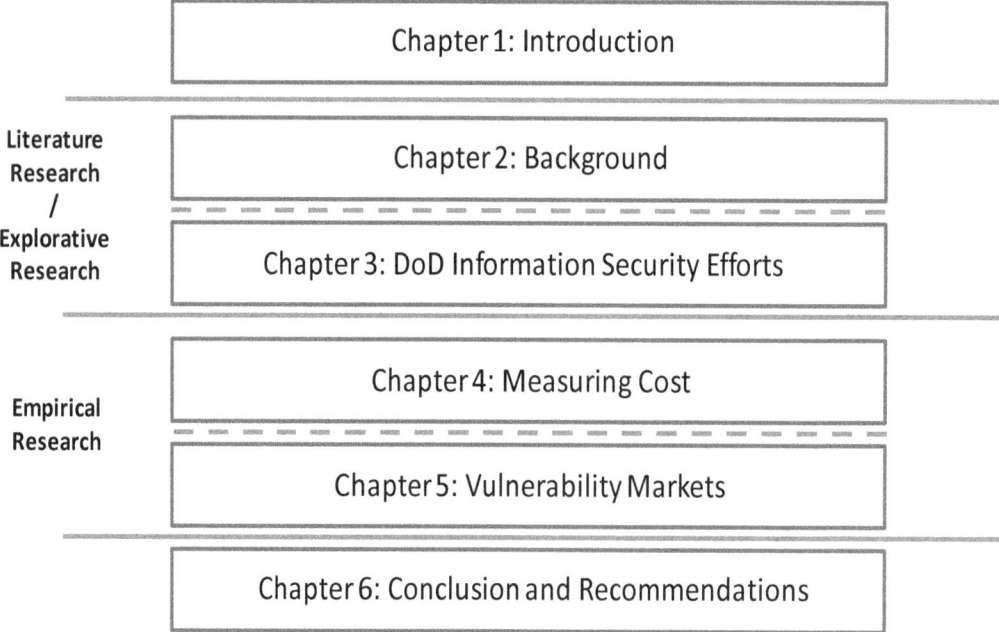

Figure 1.1 Research Methodology

The second section explores the burgeoning vulnerability market for software vulnerabilities. This section includes analysis of some of the more popular companies who stand at the forefront of vulnerability brokering. This section also consists of model analysis and the applicability of a vulnerability market in the DoD acquisition framework. Using examples from private industry and the DoD, this section will analyze a model, with validated metrics, geared at determining a comprehensive system security level. The objective of the model is to provide a quantifiable metric (e.g. Cost-to-Break) for use prior to milestone C in the DoD acquisition framework.

2. BACKGROUND

2.1 Literature Review

Prior research in software vulnerability and information assurance has focused on three major subject areas: quantifying exploitation's economic impact, predictive vulnerability discovery, and enhancing software security.

The foundation of this paper and much of the previous research done on the subject stems from the Nobel laureate, George Akerlof. In 1970, Mr. Akerlof published his seminal work "The Market for Lemons: Quality Uncertainty and the Market Mechanism" in the *Quarterly Journal of Economics* [1]. In this work, Mr. Akerlof discusses information asymmetry[4] and how the seller of a product knows more about the product than the buyer.

The emergence of cybercrime and the ability to exfiltrate information from a remote terminal caused an explosion of research related to quantifying the economic cost of cybercrime. L. Jean Camp [2], Ross Anderson et tal [3], and Rainer Böhme [4] authored several papers detailing the direct and indirect costs to the individual and society as a result of cyber crime. While the costs of cybercrime are often subjective, these works are the most detailed analyses to date.

Ross Anderson, from the University of Cambridge, applied market asymmetry to software vendors supplying insecure products to consumers [5]. Dr. Anderson was also one of the first academics to propose a software security metric with which to judge secure vs. insecure products. Taking over where Dr. Anderson left off, Dr. Stuart Schechter from Harvard University proposed a vulnerability market model for software

---

[4] Information asymmetry deals with the study of decisions in transactions where one party has more or better information than the other.

6

security testing [6]. This market model follows a Dutch auction methodology and produces a singular Cost-to-Break metric used to measure the security of a system. Finally, and the impetus of this report, Dr. Andy Ozment from Cambridge University made a clear and undisputable argument for vulnerability discovery and software security. In his doctoral dissertation, Dr. Ozment analyzed the nature of vulnerability discovery to provide insight into software security.

As of yet, no prior work has been done on the subject of enhancing the DoD and Federal acquisition process by adopting a vulnerability market for products which may impact critical assets. This paper is unique in that it provides a model to minimize risk to the DoD and heightens security of sensitive information and critical weapon systems. It is also unique as it is one of the first cost-saving models that focuses solely on DoD's cyberspace capability.

When either of the terms *cyberspace* or *cyber domain* are discussed, many people unfamiliar with this environment dismiss it as magic or mysticism. On the contrary, cyberspace and the cyber domain, are logically-governed man-made artifacts. As with any man-made artifacts, they are imperfect. The prevalence of these imperfections necessitate that DoD acquisitions play an active role in defending critical systems.

2.2 Cyberspace Vernacular

The software and network engineers who create and maintain the cyberspace environment build applications to produce a desired output. The construction of these applications revolves around logical Software Lines Of Code (SLOC). After an application is built and error-checked, the SLOC is compiled from a high-level programming language (e.g. C+, Ada, Python) into executable machine code. Once

7

compiled into an executable, all defects present in the pre-compiled program are transferred to the end product. Although the conferred defects may result in unintended and harmless manifestations for the user, some could be categorized as *vulnerabilities*.

The Defense Acquisition Guidebook defines a *vulnerability* as "any weakness in system design, development, production, or operation that can be exploited by a threat to defeat a system's mission objectives or significantly degrade its performance." [7] Example vulnerabilities include the unauthorized ability to escalate an individual's privileges, ability to overwhelm a system's buffer, or possible information leaks due to dangling pointers. While not all vulnerabilities lead to a security incursion, they all have the propensity to allow an *exploit* to be developed.

An *exploit* is entirely different from a *vulnerability*. An exploit is a malicious program that uses a discovered vulnerability to cause an information system to react with unintended behavior. Exploits may be used to access restricted data, disable or degrade a system's performance, launch other programs, monitor activity, and various other purposes. If an individual is successful in executing an exploit against a particular system, the system's security has failed and the potential damage is a function of the data managed by the information system. The key to maintaining a system's security is to identify the system's vulnerabilities before an exploit is developed. The easy solution to this conundrum is to build applications with no vulnerabilities. Unfortunately, perfect security in an application is unattainable.

2.3 The Prevalence of Vulnerabilities

Historically in the DoD, as budgets contract, information systems aggregate. This phenomenon occurs primarily to offset the expense of maintaining a large workforce by automating much of the work accomplished by soldiers, sailors, airmen, and marines. As a consequence, an increase in the number of automated processes drives an increase in the number and complexity of information systems. The negative externality associated with this phenomenon is that as the number, complexity, and size of information systems increase, the prevalence of system flaws also increase.

A common measure of the complexity of a system is calculated by enumerating the amount of software lines of codes. In 2010, a RAND study noted large code bases typically indicate a rate of one defect for every thousand lines of code. By applying this defect rate to two widely used operating systems, Windows Vista and Debian Linux, there would be approximately 50,000 defects in the Microsoft Windows Vista OS, and more than 200,000 defects in Debian Linux [8]. Applying this defect rate to the Navy DD(X)'s 10,000,000 SLOC, there may be as many as 10,000 defects. Figure 2.1 depicts additional DoD weapon systems, and their respective SLOC enumeration versus time. While only a fraction of these defects would allow access to the IS and lead to unauthorized control of the system, an entirely defect-free information system is realistically impossible to achieve.

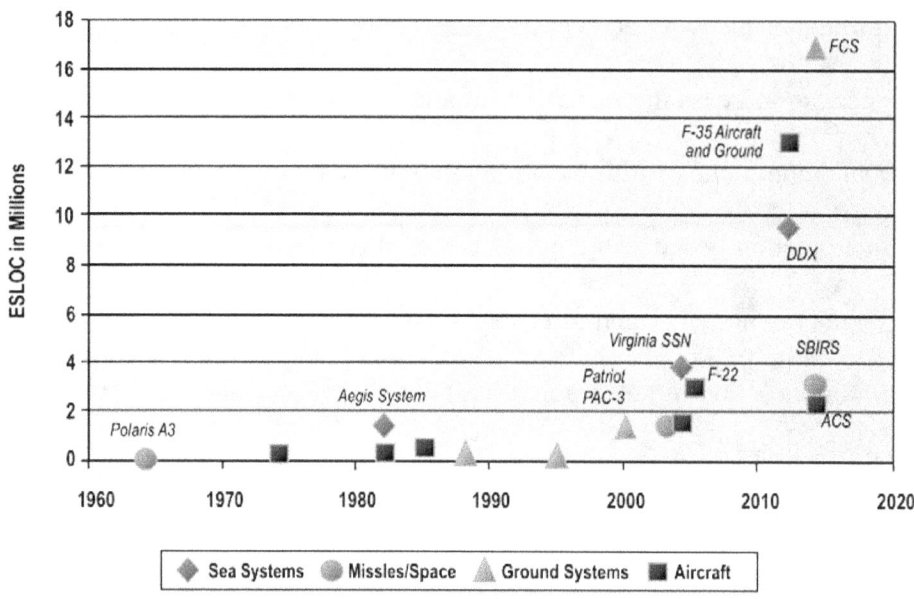

Figure 2.1 Equivalent Source Lines of Code for Selected Weapon Systems [9]

2.4 The Discovery and Reporting of Vulnerabilities

As discussed in the previous section, large and complex information systems used in the civilian and defense sectors are likely teaming with undiscovered vulnerabilities which could allow unauthorized access to malicious individuals. Fortunately for consumers, many defects and vulnerabilities are discovered during the initial beta testing prior to full system deployment. The vulnerabilities found during beta testing tend to be the "low-hanging fruit" and easiest to find using established tools and techniques. Discovery of the remaining vulnerabilities is a function of time, funds, expertise, and system exposure.

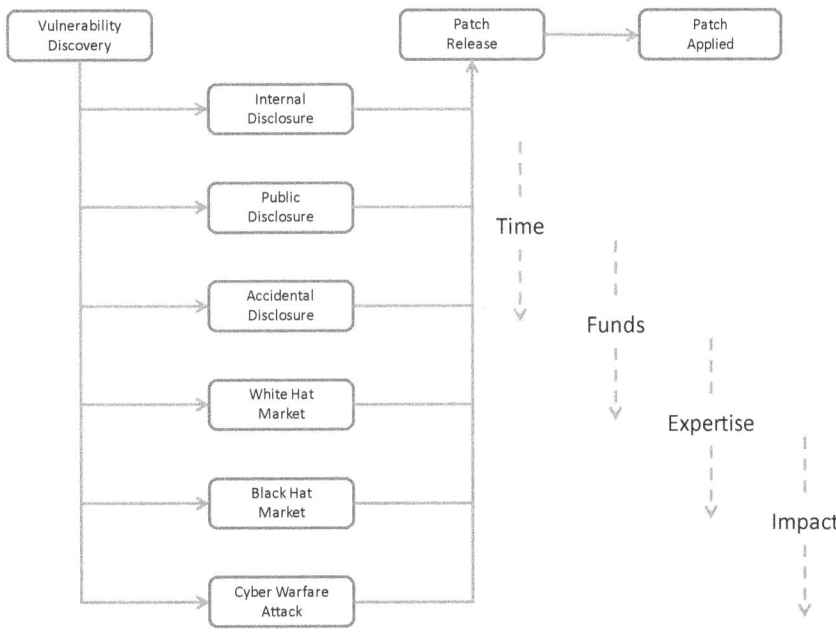

Figure 2.2 Valley of Vulnerabilities

Since the easy vulnerabilities are found and patched early on, vulnerabilities are found less frequently as the system matures. Individuals must now invest more time and money to accomplish vulnerability discovery.

Once a new vulnerability is discovered, it may be reported and patched through a variety of avenues. Referencing Figure 2.2, vulnerabilities may be reported through legitimate means, such as, internal, public, or accidental disclosure. Furthermore, vulnerabilities may be reported through illegitimate means, such as the Black Hat Market or a Cyber Attack.

2.5 Legitimate Vulnerability Reporting

In 2003, the Department of Homeland Security (DHS) established the United States Computer Emergency Readiness Team (US-CERT) to facilitate the coordination of discovered software vulnerabilities and exploits across government and industry sectors. US-CERT also coordinates with the vendors to create patches for identified security vulnerabilities. Upon discovery of the security vulnerability, the identifier contacts US-

CERT. US-CERT then contacts the vendor and establishes a deadline to release a patch for the vulnerability, after which point US-CERT releases a public advisory warning users. The vendor is responsible for producing a patch prior to release of the advisory to prevent attacks against consumers. The US-CERT provides no compensation to individuals who report system flaws nor does it levy fines against vendors who fail to accomplish patch development.

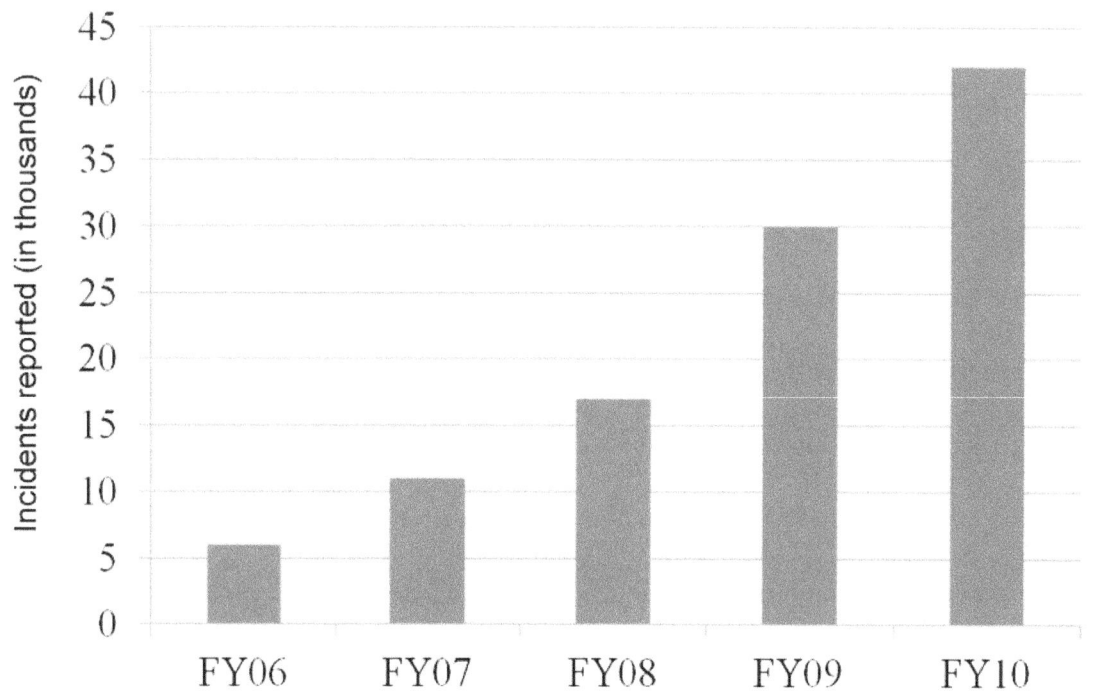

Figure 2.3 Incidents Reported to US-CERT (in thousands) [10]

With no incentives to report and little authoritative power over industry to fix, this model appears doomed to fail. On the contrary, the US-CERT program is flourishing based largely in part to an active white-hat hacker[5] community. As noted in the above Figure, US-CERT's database has grown to over 40 thousand reported vulnerabilities in

---

[5] A "white-hat" hacker refers to an ethical hacker who uses their talents to accomplish testing on an organization's information systems. "White-hat" hackers generally exercise responsible vulnerability reporting though organizations like US-CERT.

2010. [10] In addition to the DHS's US-CERT program, several software vendors are taking a proactive approach to identifying vulnerabilities in their products.

The Zero Day Initiative (ZDI) program was founded in 2005 by the network security firm, TippingPoint. The ZDI is a program that rewards researchers for finding and disclosing vulnerabilities which are then passed to product vendors. Once a vulnerability is submitted though ZDI, the Hewlett-Packard Digital Vaccine Labs (HP DVLabs) validates the vulnerability information. After validation, HP purchases it from the researcher [11]. By instituting the ZDI, TippingPoint has expanded their vulnerability lab of 48 in-house security experts to a pool of over 600 "extended researchers."

HP TippingPoint states publicly that it does not resell the reported vulnerabilities. Rather, HP submits the validated vulnerabilities to the products vendor and leaves it up to the vendor to remediate. While the vendor works on a patch for the affected product, customers of HP TippingPoint will be protected in case an exploit is developed prior to dissemination of the patched product.

Netragard established its Exploit Acquisition Program (EAP) in early 2000 in order to provide an "ethical" vehicle for researchers to submit software vulnerabilities and exploits to a vendor. Boasting a minimum payout of $20K, Netragard is one of the highest paying market sites. Much like the ZDI, the EAP provides a cash reward for reported and validated discoveries. Unlike the ZDI, Netragard states up front it intends to resell reported vulnerabilities to companies that are US-based buyers. Furthermore, eligible companies must be under contract with Netragard. Netragard established these requisites in order to prevent an accidental sale of a zero-day exploit to a hostile hacker or sale on the black market. As of August 2012, Netragard has yet to report a single software vendor contacting Netragard to purchase vulnerability information regarding their products [12]. Based on this fact, Netragard's entire revenue is dependent on third-party sales of vulnerability information.

In March 2012, Forbes magazine reported a new worldwide market for software vulnerabilities, with VUPEN being one of the biggest [13]. VUPEN, often regarded as the most vocal of the new crop of vulnerability brokers, is a France-based firm that traffics in zero-day exploits. VUPEN brags it has exploits for every major network browser and applications like Microsoft Word, Adobe Reader, and Android/iOS operating systems [14]. In a recent hacking competition sponsored by Google, VUPEN programmers successfully "pwned"[6] the Google Chrome web browser; however, they refused to release details on how the application was exploited. They refused despite being offered a $60,000 reward claiming they "wouldn't share the information with Google for even $1 million" [14].

VUPEN claims to sell exploits only to NATO governments and its partners. NATO is, however, unable to verify that all of VUPEN's transactions are legitimate or that the sold vulnerabilities are not re-sold or leaked to malicious entities.

Mailing lists, such as Bugtraq, Full Disclosure, and US-CERT, provide critical information to the software development community. The mailing lists send out automatic updates to individuals and organizations seeking to secure their networks from unauthorized intrusions and cyber attacks. These lists are U.S. government and industry sanctioned as valuable information resources regarding network security. Even though they are sanctioned and used for legitimate purposes (as is the case with many network

---

[6] "pwned" is hacker jargon derived from the verb "own". "pwn" means to compromise or control a computer, web site, gateway device, or application.

14

IDS tools), the mailing lists are also used by malicious coders. Bugtraq [15], for example, provides:

- Information on computer or network related security vulnerabilities
- Exploit programs, scripts or detailed processes.
- Patches, workarounds, fixes.
- Announcements, advisories or warnings.
- Ideas, future plans or current works dealing with computer/network security.
- Incident advisories or informational reporting.
- New or updated security tools.

While the information disseminated by these sites is useful to system security administrators, hackers also use these forums to discover reported system vulnerabilities and exploits in order to attack un-patched operating systems. These cyber criminals depend on administrators failing to update their systems as soon as the vulnerabilities are advertised. In fact, the Congressional Research Service estimates 80 percent of successful attacks use known vulnerabilities with available patches. [16]

2.6 Summary

This recent explosion of reporting tools, used for both legitimate and illegitimate purposes, is evidence that a market for vulnerability information will not lessen in significance. The Department of Defense, realizing it is not immune to the cyber attacks experienced in the public and private sectors, has issued guidance, policies, and procedures dealing with cyber security concerns. The next chapter provides an overview of the DoD's efforts to secure critical infrastructure against cyber attack.

3. DOD'S INFORMATION SECURITY EFFORTS

3.1 Introduction

DoD defines *Information Security* as "[t]he system of policies, procedures, and requirements established to protect information that, if subjected to unauthorized disclosure, could reasonably be expected to cause damage to the national security." [17] This chapter will review these information security policies, procedures, and requirements from a macro-to-micro perspective by explaining the "defense-in-depth" strategy, the DIACAP processes, and Information System information assurance testing over the acquisition lifecycle.

3.2 Defense-In-Depth

In response to the enormity and potential consequences of a state-sponsored or independent hacker exploiting critical system vulnerabilities, the DoD relies in a large part on a concept called "defense-in-depth". "Defense-in-depth" is an approach to distributing system-wide exploitation risk across multiple levels of information security. The levels that it seeks to integrate in this shared-risk environment are: "people, technology, and operations; the layering of IA solutions within and among IT assets; and, the selection of IA solutions" [18]. Stated simply, by applying information security tools across multiple boundaries of the DoD enterprise, exploiting a vulnerability at the interior of the network will be increasingly difficult.

In the physical and cyberspace domains, attack types can be categorized as targeted or indiscriminant. Indiscriminant attacks are those not focused at a particular entity, rather, they seek to exploit security vulnerabilities across many systems. These attacks are often thwarted by several layers of the DoD enterprise network security as the level of system fingerprinting[7] and malware complexity are limited and easily recognized. On the other hand, a targeted attack is executed by a highly skilled individual(s) who seek to attack a specific system. Because the target is specific, the attacker will become an expert on its network architecture, hardware and software components, and intrusion safeguards. An example of a successful and sophisticated target attack is the Stuxnet virus. The Stuxnet virus was specifically coded to affect only Siemens Simatic-S7 SCADA[8] systems. The individuals responsible for developing the Stuxnet virus spent months analyzing possible attack vectors[9], finding undiscovered vulnerabilities within the software, and also devising ways to limit collateral damage outside their specified objectives.

The defense-in-depth strategy is imperfect. As the layers of network defense increase, attack sophistication grows as well. According to an October 2011 report released by the U.S. Government Accountability Office (GAO), 20 federal agencies reported an increase in the amount of targeted and indiscriminant cyber attacks against critical information assets. In fact, these 20 federal agencies (one of which was DoD) reported a 25% increase in the number of reported intrusions from 2009 to 2010. Unlike a medieval castle where an enemy can defeat a single layer of defense without compromising the entire castle, cyber security is often defeated if a single available attack vector is successfully identified and exploited.

---

[7] Fingerprinting is the process of information gathering for a particular system.
[8] SCADA (supervisory control and data acquisition) are industrial control systems that monitor and control industrial processes.
[9] An attack vector is a path or means by which a hacker can gain access to a computer or network server in order to deliver a malicious payload (i.e. exploit).

The issues and concerns with software complexity, unknown attack vectors, and a determined advanced persistent threat necessitate that the DoD implement more rigorous information security policies and practices. Furthermore, it highlights a need for additional measures to ensure a system is as secure as possible prior to full system deployment. In an attempt to address the concerns, the DoD instituted a risk management framework called the Department of Defense Information Assurance Certification and Accreditation Process (DIACAP).

3.3 DIACAP

In November of 2007, the DoD established the DoDI 8510.01 "DoD Information Assurance Certification and Accreditation Process (DIACAP)" policy. The purpose of DIACAP is to provide a risk management process for IA and detail information system certification and accreditation requirements throughout a system's lifecycle. It provides a step-by-step process to assure DoD systems are protected and defended "by ensuring their availability, integrity, authentication, confidentiality, and non-repudiation" [18]. DIACAP was created out of necessity because the former policy, DITSCAP[10], focused more on standalone systems and was ill-equipped to handle information systems in a network environment. Improving upon DITSCAP, DIACAP established information assurance controls which are standardized across all DoD components.

The IA controls dictate the level of required security based upon mission assurance criticality and Confidentiality Level (CL) for each IS connected to DoD networks (reference Table 3.1). The Mission Assurance Category (MAC) and confidentiality levels of an IS are system specific and based upon the mission each system is designed to

---

[10] DITSCAP is the DoD Information Technology Security Certification and Accreditation Process (DoD Instruction 5200.40) which was superseded by DIACAP in 2007.

accomplish. For example, an IS involved in generating a time-sensitive targeting solution

may be categorized a MAC I classified (the most restrictive) system; an unclassified web

portal may be categorized a MAC III public system (for more detailed descriptions, see

appendix A). Once a system is assigned a MAC and a CL, the system owner identifies

the IA controls[11] within DoDI 8510.01 that the system must achieve prior to connecting

to the network. This policy was a huge leap forward in protecting the DoD information

system enterprise from malicious cyber attacks. Every department now has a standard set

of rules for the governance of IA controls, a schedule to review an individual system's IA

status, and testable metrics to measure security effectiveness.

Table 3.1 DIACAP MAC and CL Categories [19]

Mission Assurance Categories			
Level	Definition	Integrity	Availability
1	Vital to operational readiness or mission effectiveness of deployed or contingency forces. Loss of integrity or availability unacceptable. Requires most stringent protective measures.	High	High
2	Important to the support of deployed or contingency forces. Loss of integrity unacceptable, unavailability tolerable only for short time. Require additional safeguards beyond best practices.	High	Medium
3	Necessary to conduct of day-to-day business. Protection commensurate with commercial best practices.	Basic	Basic

Confidentiality Levels	
Level	Definition
Classified	Systems processing classified information
Sensitive	Systems processing sensitive information as defined in DoDD 8500.1, to include any unclassified information not cleared for public release
Public	Systems processing publicly releasable information as defined in DoDD 8500.1 (i.e., information that has undergone a security review and been cleared for public release)

Although this is seen as an improvement over its predecessor, DIACAP has flaws.

As stated above, DIACAP measures security effectiveness according to a prescribed

---

[11] An IA control describes an objective IA condition achieved through the application of specific safeguards or through the regulation of specific activities. DIACAP also requires that an objective IA condition be testable, have a measurable compliance metric, and the activities required to achieve the IA control are accountable to an individual. To find the complete list of IA controls required for a system, reference DoDI 8510.01.

timeline (every one to two years). Should a new vulnerability be discovered, verification of security patch installation could then take months before the next IA inspection. Furthermore, the IA controls monitor known system vulnerabilities and do not take into account threat monitoring, incident detection, or incident response. For example, DIACAP requires that some systems have an Intrusion Detection System (IDS) attached to their network. The IDS, however, does not measure the ability of the system administrators in reacting to an intrusion. Rather, the IDS simply alerts the system administrators of possible malicious network activity.

DIACAP is a risk mitigation process which is more reactive than proactive when it comes to system vulnerabilities. It works well for new IS acquisitions as they are tested against the latest vulnerability database with the latest tools. As systems mature, DIACAP becomes less effective as threat monitoring takes a back seat to operations.

3.4 Information Assurance Testing

Prior to a new information system acquisition being fielded, it must first undergo DT&E and OT&E[12]. Embedded within these two acquisition milestones, DoDI 5000.02, "Operation of the Defense Acquisition System," directs that information assurance test and evaluation be accomplished to ensure system requirements are met. With respect to vulnerability discovery, the DoD uses penetration testing to ensure an IS is secure against known vulnerabilities.

Penetration testing[13], or authorized hacking, is designed to evaluate the vulnerability of a system to indiscriminant and targeted cyber attacks. The goal of the penetration testers is to obtain unauthorized privileges by exploiting flaws in system design or

---

[12] DT&E (Developmental Test and Evaluation) and OT&E (Operational Test and Evaluation)
[13] Popular applications for penetration testing includes Canvas, Core Impact, Nessus, Nmap, Metasploit

20

implementation [20]. Other incidents that penetration testing detects include denials of service and malware infections. Unfortunately, penetration testing can never prove a system is void of vulnerabilities. Penetration testing only identifies the presence of known vulnerabilities.

Following the fielding decision for an IS, organizations may also schedule periodic red and blue team[14] penetration exercises to test system security. These tests are proven effective across the entire DoD network; however, team manpower makes it difficult to assess a majority of systems. In an effort to offset the manpower shortfall, the DoD is embarking on the development of several "cyber test ranges" to simulate real world conditions in a controlled environment.

In accordance with the Comprehensive National Security Initiative (CNCI), DoD is constructing cyber test ranges to test technical and operational concepts. Specifically, the CNCI tasked the DoD to "establish a front line of defense against today's immediate threats by creating or enhancing…the ability to act quickly to reduce our current vulnerabilities and prevent intrusions." [21] Two such ranges in development are known as the DoD Information Assurance Range (IAR) and the National Cyber Range (NCR).

The DISA managed IAR models the Global Information Grid and its IA/computer network defense capabilities. Focused on the macro-level of the DoD network, the IAR is capable of executing scripted scenarios that mitigate an advanced persistent threat (APT) attempts to intercept, deny, or degrade operations. The second range in development is DARPA's NCR. Supporting the DoD and other federal agencies, the NCR emulates large-scale networks found in the real-world cyber environment. Both

---

[14] In these types of exercises, the organization is only aware of blue team activities. Red team executes clandestine intrusion attempts.

ranges are optimized to determine the impacts of large-scale indiscriminate cyber attacks and have limited ability to model targeted attacks against specific systems.

3.5 Summary

The assemblage of the DoD defense-in-depth strategy, DIACAP framework, penetration test tools, and cyber test ranges represents the government's dedication to identify known system vulnerabilities. Even with these monumental fiscal and personnel investments, the DoD remains susceptible to network attacks due to new vulnerability disclosures, patch release timelines, complex architectures, and supply chain vulnerabilities.

So far, this paper has briefly described the science of vulnerability disclosure and reporting, the vulnerability economy, and DoD efforts to secure its network. The next chapter deals with how an organization can determine the financial impact of a network attack due to an exploited vulnerability. It will also address how the early identification and remediation of an unknown vulnerability will lower a system's exposure to a malicious hacker.

4. MEASURING THE COST OF A CYBER ATTACK

4.1 Introduction

How does the DoD calculate the cost of a cyber attack? This question is not easily answered as there are many factors that determine total cost. In 2011, a global network security powerhouse, McAfee, reported the global economic impact to cyber attacks is as large as $1 trillion dollars. Furthermore, General Keith Alexander, commander of USCYBERCOM and Director of the National Security Agency (NSA), estimated that the U.S. loses $250 billion annually to cybercriminals. While a detailed account on how these estimates were formulated is not available, the public can assume the estimates were built using the following categories:

1. **Costs in anticipation of a cyber attack.** Include the DoD's investment in the cyber security architecture (such as installing and implementing the defense-in-depth strategy).

2. **Costs as a consequence of a cyber attack.** Takes into account the direct losses to an individual, service, defense industrial base, and overall national security.

3. **Indirect costs associated with a cyber attack.** Includes damage to an organization's reputation, loss in national confidence, and time required to recover. [22]

In the civilian sector, costs are enumerated by the number of credit card numbers stolen, intellectual property theft, and pilfered insider trading information. In the defense sector, costs are measured as impacts to operations and intelligence theft. The value of these stolen items or impact to operations is dependent on discrete events in time. For example, a Denial of Service (DoS) attack on a system during a military engagement will

23

cost more than the same DoS attack on that exact system during peacetime. Based on the complexity of devising costs for a cyber attacks, this paper will generalize "cost" by calculating a probabilistic outcome using expected values[15]. By calculating expected values this paper will estimate possible savings and produce a cost-benefit analysis.

4.2 Defining the Basic Formulas

In an effort to identify how the vulnerability market can strengthen overall system security, some basic formulas used to model the risk of a system to a particular vulnerability will be defined. For this analysis, this paper uses the Single Loss Expectancy (SLE) formula to calculate the expected loss due to an exploited vulnerability.

4.2.1 Single Loss Expectancy

The Single Loss Expectancy (SLE) calculates a monetary value based on the occurrence of a risk on a system. Calculating the SLE for a system incorporates two factors: the value of the at-risk asset (AV) and the asset's Exposure Factor (EF). The Exposure Factor is a percentage of the asset's value that will be lost in the case of an attack. In the DoD, quantifying AV is difficult as it should include the value of information, value of lost productivity, the value of remediation, and (in extreme cases) the value of human life.

Suppose the DoD has an information technology asset (A) which is vulnerable to a particular system vulnerability (j). Let AV be the value of A and let EF_j be the exposure factor for asset A when A is successfully attacked through the vulnerability j.

---

[15] "Expected Value" of a random variable (cost) is the weighted average (probabilities) of all possible values that this random variable can take on.

Furthermore, let P_j be the probability of a successful attack on A through the vulnerability j. Incorporating these variables a successful attack will result in the following:

$$Single\ Loss\ Expectancy\ (SLE) = (AV \times EF_j) \times P_j$$

For this discussion, consider the following example.

A financial MAC III system, *System_A*, is deployed to three system program offices (SPO) at the Electronic Systems Center (ESC) at Hanscom AFB. This system stores budgetary data for the current and future fiscal year execution for the three SPOs. DoD informed ESC that *System_A* possesses a particular system vulnerability that would cause a catastrophic loss of data. Each of these SPOs has a contingency plan where loss of *System_A* would require that all financial transactions use a backup system. Utilization of this backup system results in a 50% loss of productivity. Furthermore, loss of *System_A* would erase all current and historical financial databases requiring significant rework. According to current estimates of a total loss of *System_A*, it would take four weeks to get the system back online. Moreover, the ESC estimates that a system vulnerability exploit would only impact two SPOs before the third is isolated from attack. Based upon historical cyber attack rates, the probability that this particular vulnerability be exploited is 15%.

Table 4.1 Quantitative Measurements: *System_A*

Asset Valuation Components	Value	Justification
Direct Costs		
Inventory	$100,000	Financial Databases
System Restoration	$50,000	Cost to repair *System_A* to full operational capability
Indirect Costs		
Lost Productivity	$200,000	Lost productivity due to time to remediate system loss
Database Restoration	$50,000	Time require to rebuild financial databases
Program Delays	$300,000	Impact of productivity loss to the four programs the office administers.
Total Asset Value	**$700,000**	

Using this example, first begin identifying the direct and indirect cost associated with the loss of *System_A*. These costs are depicted above in Table 4.1. Furthermore, for the SLE to be calculated, the average amount of loss to the asset for a single incident must be determined. In this example, the EF experienced by the entire system is 0.667, because only two of the three program offices would be affected by a system outage. Applying the SLE formula for this example, the SLE for this cyber attack is:

Single Loss Expectancy = $700,000 x 0.667 x 0.15 = $70,035

The resultant SLE is the monetary risk that the organization incurs by not mitigating the probability of a particular vulnerability being exploited. Assuming an asset's value remains constant, the SLE can be reduced by either lowering the exposure factor or the probability of a successful attack. The government reduces these two variables by making smart investments. The expected benefit of these smart investments is outlined in the next section.

4.2.2 Expected Benefit

As stated above, P_j is the probability of a successful attack on an asset (A) through a system vulnerability j. If P_j is equal to 0, then the asset is assumed to be impervious to the vulnerability. Conversely, if P_j is equal to 1, the asset is completely exposed. Therefore, if P_j is greater than 0, DoD has the opportunity to make an investment to reduce the system's vulnerability and expected losses from a cyber attack.

Assume the DoD makes an investment *i* that makes the asset (A) more secure from vulnerability j. The new probability is now annotated as P_j^i. By including this new investment into the SLE formula above, the expected benefit of investing in *i* is:

Expected Benefit of i = (AV × EF$_j$) × [P$_j$ - P$_j^i$]

26

Using this expected benefit formula and factoring in the cost for the investment *Price$_i$*, the expected net benefit for investing in *Price$_i$* is:

$$\textbf{\textit{Expected Net Benefit of i = (AV × EF$_j$) × [P$_j$ - P$_j^i$]- Price$_i$}}$$

Interpreting the calculated value from the *expected net benefit of i*, a positive result translates into a beneficial investment.

4.2.3 Total Expected Loss

It is unrealistic to believe a system in the DoD inventory is only susceptible to a single vulnerability. In fact (and as outlined in Chapter 2.3), a DoD system could have hundreds or thousands of vulnerabilities (known and unknown). To account for the entire set of vulnerabilities against a particular system, the Total Expected Loss for the set of all possible vulnerabilities $\{T_j\}$ is the summation of Single Loss Expectancies.

4.3 Quantitative Analysis

Now that the basic formulas are defined, the next task is to model a system's total expected loss as the sum of possible SLEs (e.g. $SLE_1 + SLE_2 + SLE_3 + \ldots + SLE_n$). The sum of system SLEs can be stated as:

$$Total\ Expected\ Loss\ (TEL) = \sum_{j=1}^{n} SLE_j = \sum_{j=1}^{n} (AV \times EF_j) \times P_j$$

SLE_j is the total expected loss of an asset, A, due to the exploitation of system vulnerability, j. For this given system, there are a total of *n* vulnerabilities. Now assume that the DoD engages in a strategy in which a set of vulnerabilities $\{U_j\}$ are discovered and fixed prior to system deployment. Set $\{U_j\}$ is a subset of $\{T_j\}$. By integrating this set of purchased vulnerabilities, the new total expected loss equation is:

$$TEL' = \left[\sum_{j \in T_j} (AV \times EF_j) \times P_j \right] - \left[\sum_{j \in U_j} (AV \times EF_j) \times P_j \right] - \sum_{j \in U_j} Price_j$$

This set of purchased vulnerabilities $\{U_j\}$ effectively removes each corresponding SLE by changing the probability of attack from P_j to 0. Since $\{Uj\}$ is a subset of $\{Tj\}$, the difference between the two summations is a positive value. As long as the cost of the purchased vulnerabilities ($Price_j$) is less than the difference, the expected net benefit is positive.

Applying the above formula to historical vulnerability disclosures, the potential expected net benefit of a product using a vulnerability market prior to product release may be simulated.

4.4 Vulnerability Discovery Phases

The lifecycle of an information system typically consists of three common phases: *learning*, *linear*, and *saturation* (see Figure 4.1) [40]. These phases are important as vulnerability discovery rates increase and decrease over time as the system passes through each window. The *learning* phase occurs immediately after the system is released to the public. During this phase, researchers and hackers become familiar with the system and gain better knowledge on how to break it. As a result of this lack of system knowledge, the vulnerability discovery rate during this phase tends to be low. Following the learning phase, the *linear* phase is characterized by a linear growth of vulnerabilities discovered by users. This explosion of discoveries is due to the system gaining market penetration and an increase in system familiarity. Once the system

28

reaches obsolescence or as the number of unknown vulnerabilities diminish, the

vulnerability rate reduces as more users convert to a replacement and hackers lose

interest. During this time the system is experiencing the *saturation* phase.

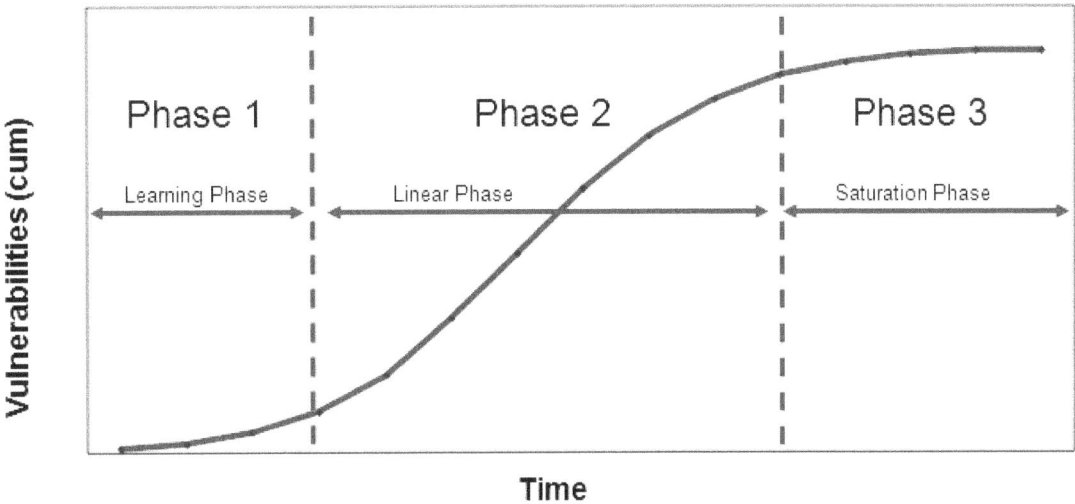

Figure 4.1 Vulnerability Disclosure Rate Phases [40]

The length of time a system experiences each of the phases varies greatly. For

example, if the hackers adapt to the new system quickly, the learning phase is short-lived.

Furthermore, if the system is rife with vulnerabilities, the saturation phase may never be

seen. Examples of these phases are readily seen in the commercial market. For analysis

purposes, three popular systems are chosen: Adobe Acrobat, the Java Development Kit

(JDK), and Windows XP.

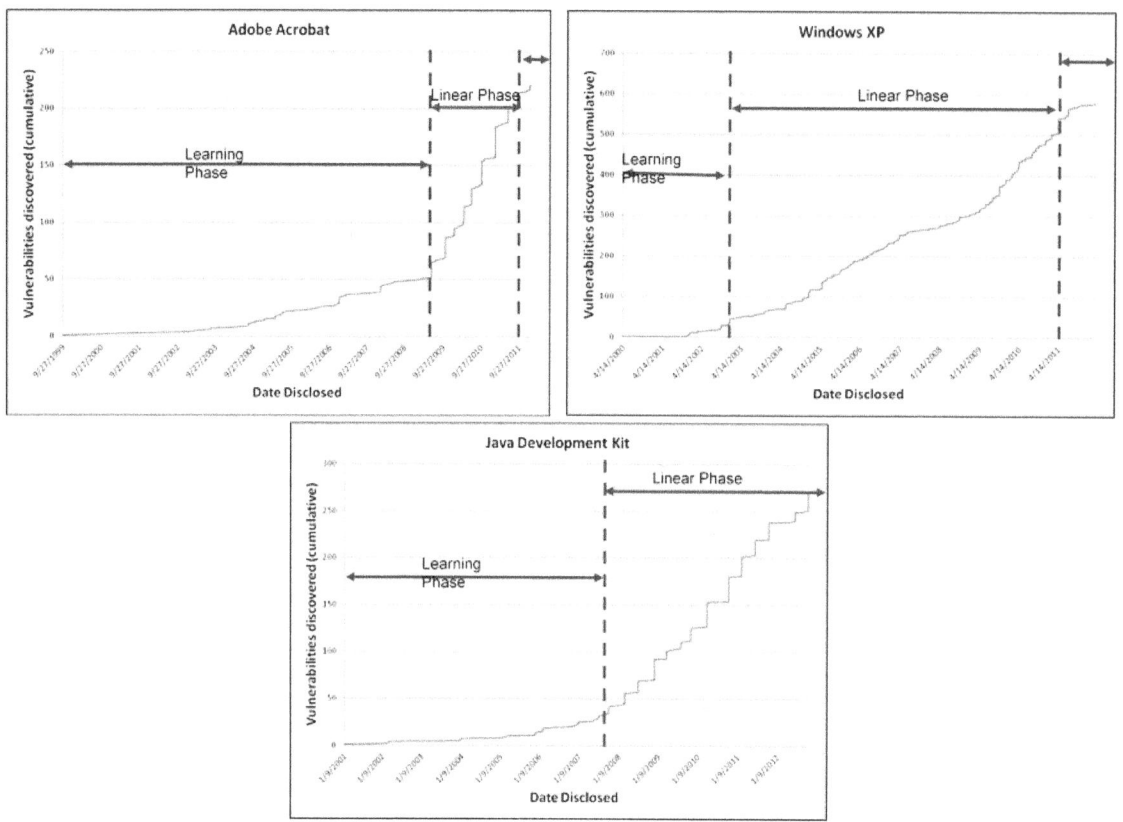

Figure 4.2 Vulnerability Disclosure Histories (Adobe Acrobat, Windows XP, JDK)[16]

As evident in Figure 4.2, there are clear delineations between the *learning* and *linear* phases. Also of note is the variability of phase lengths between software systems. Windows XP's learning phase was approximately three years where Adobe Acrobat experienced a 10-year learning phase. The causal factor of this variability is based on market share. For the Windows XP operating system, consumers quickly upgraded from the obsolete Windows 98/NT systems. The quick conversion ensured that Windows XP gained a large share of the market over a relatively short amount of time. In contrast, the Adobe Acrobat's share of the Portable Document Format (PDF) market was limited by competitor saturation. It wasn't until July 2003 and the release of Adobe version 6.0 that

---

[16] Data on these systems was acquired from the CVE details website http://www.cvedetails.com/.

the system gained popularity over similar proprietary systems. Shortly after 2003, Adobe

Acrobat entered the *linear* phase.

While the Common Vulnerabilities and Exposures database allows historical trend

analysis, researchers have been searching for a model which will allow for predictive

study. One such model is the Alhazmi-Malaiya Logistic (AML) model [40]. The AML

model assumes that the shape of the vulnerability curve is restricted by market share and

the number of the undiscovered vulnerabilities[17]. The model proposes that the

vulnerability discovery rate is given by the following differential equation:

$$\frac{d\Omega}{dt} = A\Omega\,(B - \Omega) \tag{1}$$

The two factors in equation (1), $A\Omega$ and $(B - \Omega)$, relate to the application's market

share and the number of system vulnerabilities. $A\Omega$ increases as market share increases

and $(B - \Omega)$ decreases as the number of available vulnerabilities (B) decrease. Solving for

$\Omega(t)$, the following logarithmic equation is produced:

$$\Omega(t) = \frac{B}{BCe^{-ABt} + 1} \tag{2}$$

In this equation, as time (t) approaches infinity, $\Omega(t)$ approaches B. Assuming the

other variables remain constant, decreasing the number of vulnerabilities in a system (B)

would flatten the shape of the s-curve. This behavior is observed in Figure 4.3. Stating

that the market share ($A\Omega$) remains constant is appropriate for DoD. More often than

not, DoD acquires a specific application or system to meet a specified mission.

Consequently, that system has a constant market share within the DoD. As a DoD

---

[17] Subsequent discussion and equations are taken from [40]

31

system becomes obsolete and replaced, there is a resultant transition time; however, it has

an accelerated pace which limits the *saturation* phase.

From its initial release in April of 1999 to April 2012, the Adobe Acrobat application

has had a total of 246 vulnerabilities reported to the CVE database, Bugtraq mailing list,

and US-CERT. The cumulative number of vulnerabilities over time is depicted in Figure

4.3.

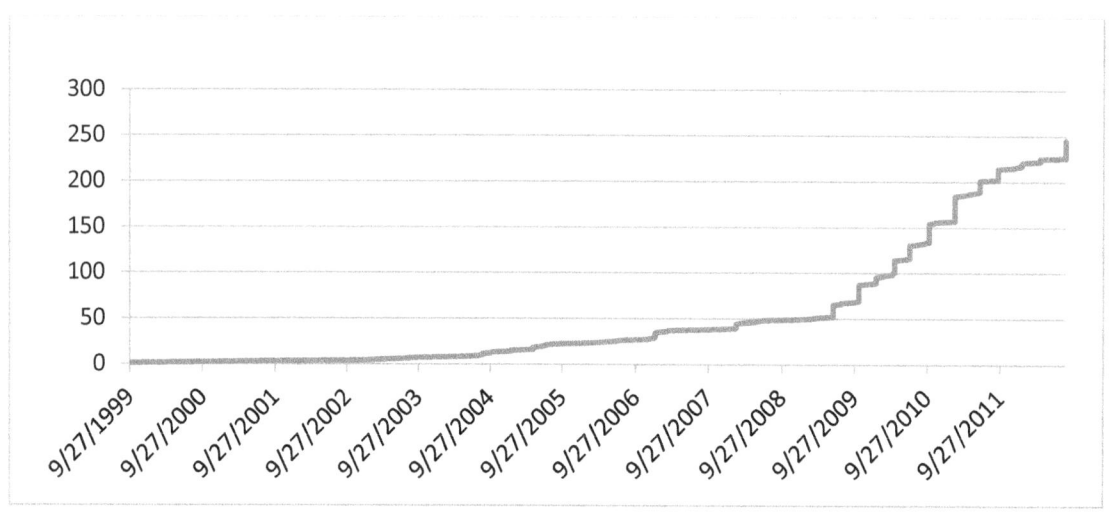

Figure 4.3 Vulnerability Disclosure Rate for Adobe Acrobat[18]

To analyze the Adobe Acrobat dataset, several assumptions are necessary. First of

all, because the asset value of the application is unknown, a fixed cost will be assigned

and remain constant. Second, the application's exposure factor will be calculated using

the National Vulnerability Database (NVD)[19] Common Vulnerability Scoring System

(CVSS). Third, the analysis assumes that the cost of each vulnerability against the

system is constant (e.g. $V_1 = V_{1+n} \in \{V_{1...m}\}$) and that the cost of a vulnerability is greater

than 0.

---

[18] Statistics derived from the CVE vulnerability database.
[19] The National Vulnerability Database (NVD) is maintained by the National Institute of Standards and Technology.

The CVSS score for a vulnerability details possible *impact* to a systems confidentiality[20], integrity[21], and availability[22]. Furthermore, the CVSS score incorporates the *exploitability* of a system to a specific vulnerability by factoring in the access vector[23], access complexity[24], and requirement for authentication[25]. The equations for how CVSS quantifies these two metrics are detailed in the Table below.

Table 4.2 CVSS Equations [10]

AccessVector = case AccessVector of
        requires local access: 0.395
        adjacent network accessible: 0.646
        network accessible: 1.0

AccessComplexity = case AccessComplexity of
        high: 0.35
        medium: 0.61
        low: 0.71

Authentication= case Authentication of
        requires multiple instances of authentication: 0.45
        requires single instance of authentication: 0.56
        requires no authentication: 0.704

ConfImpact   = case ConfidentialityImpact of
        none: 0.0
        partial: 0.275
        complete: 0.660

IntegImpact   = case IntegrityImpact of
        none: 0.0
        partial: 0.275
        complete: 0.660

AvailImpact   = case AvailabilityImpact of
        none: 0.0
        partial: 0.275
        complete: 0.660

---

[20] Confidentiality: Assurance that information is not disclosed to unauthorized entities or processes.
[21] Integrity: Protection against unauthorized modification or destruction of information.
[22] Availability: Timely, reliable access to data and information services for authorized users.
[23] Access Vector reflects how the vulnerability is exploited.
[24] Access Complexity measures the complexity of the attack required to exploit the vulnerability.
[25] Authentication measures the number of times an attacker must authenticate to exploit a vulnerability.

In order to estimate a system's exposure factor (EF), this analysis used the product of the *impact* and *exploitability* CVSS values for a known vulnerability. Furthermore, to simulate the probability of a system attack using a known vulnerability, this exercise assumes equal likelihood across the entire data set. Otherwise stated, each discovered vulnerability has an equal probability of being used to exploit the system.

Using the source data from the CVSS database, the Total Expected Loss formula, and varying the vulnerability discovery rates, vulnerability remediation costs significantly reduce the overall lifecycle costs for the application (see Figure 4.4).

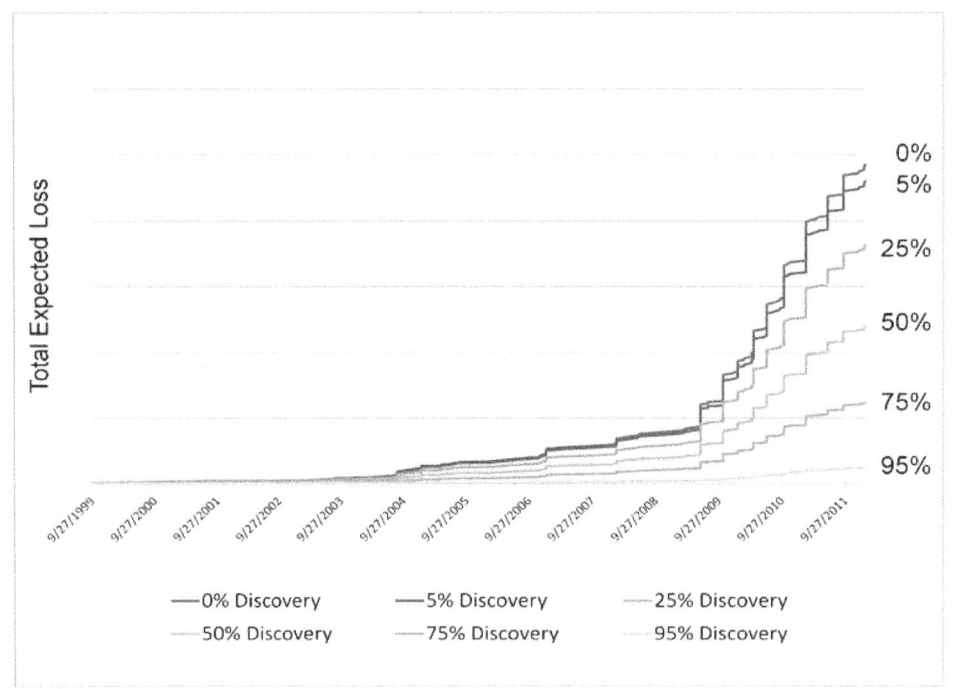

Figure 4.4 Impact of Vulnerability Discovery before Release

This exercise conclusively proves that if a vulnerability is found prior to system deployment, overall lifecycle costs are reduced. As seen above, cost reductions to Total Expected Loss depends primarily upon vulnerability discovery rates. Based on this conclusion, the DoD should focus on developing a mechanism which promotes vulnerability disclosure. The following chapter (Chapter 5) will discuss how a

34

vulnerability market can assist in increasing the vulnerability discovery rate to maximize savings.

4.5 Quantitative Analysis Advantages and Disadvantages

The primary advantage of conducting such a quantitative analysis is that the organization will introduce objectivity into the risk mitigation process. As a result of using established formulas to determine the probability and impact of an exploited vulnerability, the resultant value can be determined as objective and void of subjective influence. Furthermore, by using the predetermined formulas, both the impact of a single loss and expected net benefit can be expressed in terms easily understood by decision makers (e.g. U.S. dollars). In turn, the values calculated could be used for further statistical analysis and support budget decisions.

Unfortunately, this process has some disadvantages. Although SLE and EV are computed via quantitative formulas, the exposure factor and asset value variables are subjective measurements based on the particular asset. This disadvantage results in complex valuations which may not be understood by officials obligating funds for information security. Moreover, collecting information to derive the value of the asset is labor intensive and requires consensus across all stakeholders.

The largest single shortfall of this risk assessment methodology is assigning a probability that a vulnerability will be used to exploit the system. DoD does not keep scientifically valid statistics upon which to base the P_j estimates. To mitigate this shortfall, several promising models are available to estimate a system vulnerability discovery rate (see Figure 4.5).

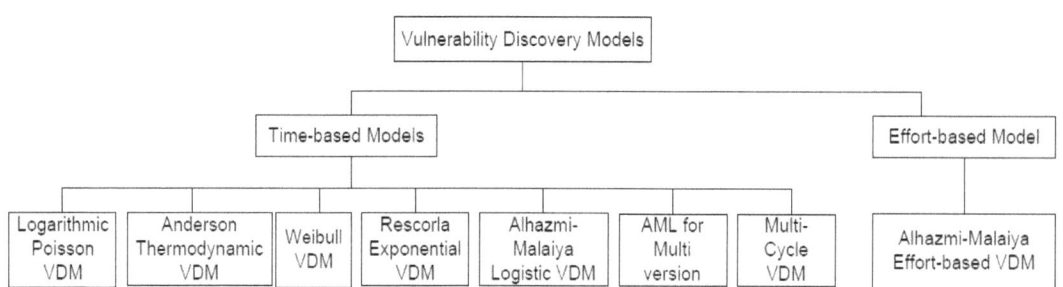

Figure 4.5 Vulnerability Discovery Models [23]

While the vulnerability discovery models provide an estimate for vulnerability disclosures, they still lack in predicting the impact a particular vulnerability would have on a system. With this limitation, and until a realistic prediction model surfaces, attack probabilities remain subjective.

5. VULNERABILITY MARKETS

5.1 Introduction

Prior to 1997, the Federal Acquisition Regulation (FAR) prohibited the use of auctions to establish contracts between the government and supplier. Language in the FAR 15.610(e)(2) specifically prohibited auction techniques that indicate to an offeror a cost that it must meet to obtain further consideration; advise an offeror of its price standing relative to another offeror; and otherwise furnish information about other offerors' prices [24]. In 1997, the FAR was rewritten and the Office of Management and Budget (OMB) removed the ban on government involvement in auctions. Ever since, DoD has taken advantage of the e-commerce auction marketplace to procure a variety of supplies. Examples of DoD auction procurements include:

- The Navy procuring airplane and ship parts.
- The Army purchasing IBM ThinkPads, saving 40 percent off the GSA price.
- The Army purchased spare parts for the Patriot Missile system.
- The Air Force used online auctions to acquire computer equipment to save $88,000 (or 27 percent of the estimated cost) in August 2002. [25]

In these tight fiscal times, where saving money is the lifeblood of any program, the possible savings achieved by using online auctions is hard to ignore. Thus far, however, these auctions have only been employed for the procurement of physical items and never aimed towards purchasing software security vulnerabilities in the cyber domain.

As with any physical item procured by DoD, Information Systems must meet reliability, maintainability, and availability requirements that can be verified in a testable environment. In the DoD, these requirements are referred to as Key Performance

37

Parameters, or KPPs[26]. This chapter will expand on the usage of the vulnerability market to procure cyber vulnerability reports while focusing on the need to meet customer requirements and reduce costs across the entire lifecycle.

5.2 Vulnerability Market Examples

As documented in Chapter 2.5, the technology community saw an explosion of vulnerability markets in the past decade. The vulnerability market, or the market for zero-day exploits[27], emerged as a way for security researchers and hackers to disclose vulnerabilities for financial gain. In the past decade, three vulnerability markets model surfaced which form the majority of vulnerability events. They are the bug challenge, the bug bounty, and the bug auction.

5.2.1 Bug Challenge

In a bug challenge, the simplest of the vulnerability market models, a vendor offers a reward for the reporting vulnerabilities related to a particular product. Unlike the other two models described below, the bug challenge is administered directly by vendor and has no intermediary to act as a clearinghouse. This model has a couple major flaws. First of all, prizes for a vulnerability are not market-driven and may not accurately reflect its actual value. [26] Because finding a security vulnerability involves a significant investment, the researcher could sell his find on the black vulnerability market for a much higher price. Secondly, bug challenges are often by invitation-only where the researchers are placed on contract and required to sign non-disclosure agreements. By restricting the researcher, the vendor has the ability to keep a vulnerability secret and refuse to patch the

---

[26] Key Performance Parameters (KPPs) are those attributes or characteristics of a system that are considered critical or essential to the development of an effective military capability.
[27] A zero-day exploit takes advantage of a software vulnerability for where there is no patch. The term "zero-day" refers to the first day that a vulnerability is discovered.

product. These two deficiencies in the model can limit the effectiveness of a bug challenge. It has, however, had some success.

For three weeks in 2000, the Secure Digital Music Initiative (SDMI) conducted a public challenge aimed at breaking SDMI watermarking[28] technologies. The challenge was invitation-only and offered a small cash prize for any team that could win any of the six challenges posed. The ultimate goal was to identify an authentic copy of the audio file to combat online music piracy. This event was sanctioned by the music recording industry and required all participants to sign a nondisclosure agreement prior to accessing SDMI data files [27].

5.2.2 Bug Bounties

Differing from a bug challenge, a bug bounty is conducted by a vendor seeking to pay researchers to identify malicious code used to infiltrate their systems. The goal of this market model is to flush out an undetected (by the vendor) vulnerability currently being exploited by hackers. Placing a bounty on vulnerabilities is, by nature, a reactive countermeasure to software lack of security.

Recognizing the benefit of this model, the company that developed the popular web browser Mozilla instituted the Mozilla Security Bug Bounty. Starting in 2004 [28], the Bug Bounty sought to reward individuals who reported *critical* security bugs. Since December of 2010, Mozilla has paid out a total of $104,000 for 64 qualifying bugs. Other companies do not pay researchers for vulnerability discoveries; however, some establish Anti-Virus Rewards programs.

---

[28] Watermarking is the process of encoding data into a audio file without a perceptible change in how the file sounds.

Microsoft's Anti-Virus Rewards program was established in 2003 and designed to "help law enforcement agencies identify and bring to justice those who illegally release damaging worms, viruses and other types of malicious code on the Internet."[29] Microsoft is known for rewarding third parties up to $250,000 for information on worms such as Blaster, SoBig and MyDoom which caused an estimate $35 million in damages. Differentiating itself from Mozilla's program, Microsoft is not paying others for identifying vulnerabilities. The Anti-Virus program is aimed at punishing those that exploit previously discovered vulnerabilities.

5.2.3 Bug Auctions

A bug auction utilizes auction theory to conduct a vulnerability market. Conducted in an online environment, sellers of vulnerabilities attempt to maximize profit while buyers attempt to minimize cost. In bug auctions, two models are commonly used: the English and Dutch auctions (ref Table 5.1).

Table 5.1 Description of Common Auction Types [25]

Auction Type	Bidding / Offer Process	Description
English (Traditional)	Bids increase	This is the typical auction in which a single seller of a single item (or lot of items) receives increasing bids from prospective buyers. The auction ends at a predetermined time, and the item goes to the highest bidder for the highest bid price.
Dutch (Reverse)	Offers decrease	The opposite of the English auction. A single buyer of a single item (or lot of items) receives decreasing offers from prospective sellers. The auction ends at a predetermined time, and the item is purchased from lowest offerer for the lowest price.

In December of 2005, an individual, under the handle "fearwall", opened an online English vulnerability auction to sell a Microsoft backdoor vulnerability. The malicious code allowed a user to create an Excel file that takes control of a computer running the Windows operating system. The auction was hosted on the well known and freely accessible auction site eBay.com. After complaints by Microsoft, eBay cancelled the auction stating that fearwall violated company policy by "promoting illegal activity". [30]

While the auction was not illegal, Microsoft objected to the vulnerability sale because it undermined trust in their product and could impact stock valuations. The auction was initially opened at $0.01 (seller hoped to receive $1200[29]) and quickly grew to approximately $56 before the auction was removed from the site. [31] Had Microsoft initiated the auction by looking for a vulnerability in Excel and willing to pay for information, this auction would have been seen as a legitimate enterprise.

In contrast to the standard English auction, Dutch (reverse) auctions are common. Reverse auctions, consisting of one buyer and multiple sellers, are gaining a foothold in government material acquisitions. While not yet applied to information security, several federal agencies recognize the financial benefit of market competition between suppliers. Several cases of successful reverse auctions are detailed in the Table below.

---

[29] Fearwall offered Microsoft employees a 10% discount if they held the winning bid for the excel vulnerability.

Table 5.2 Historic Savings from Commercial and Government Auctions [32]

Procuring Activity	Item Procured	Cost Savings	% Savings
State of PA	Aluminum	$170,000	9%
United Technology	Circuit Boards	$32,000,000	53%
Owens Corning	Packing Materials	$7,000,000	7%
US Navy -NAVCIP	Ejection Seat Components	$933,000	28%
USAF	Computers	$88,000	27%
DESC	Natural Gas	$972,000	22%
US Army CECOM	Transformers	$195,000	53%

Reverse auctions have the propensity to benefit DoD information security in multiple ways. First, reverse auctions will enhance cyber security through the identification of vulnerabilities prior to a hacker exploiting the system. Secondly, the auctions will leverage the skills and knowledge of private security researchers in the private sector. Finally, when compared to an expected loss, executing an auction costs far less than remediating an attack. Based on these advantages, this paper will concentrate on developing a reverse auction model to be used by the DoD prior to full system deployment.

5.3 Applying Reverse Auctions to the DoD Information System Acquisition Process

In 2004, Dr. Andy Ozment, from the University of Cambridge, proposed a model that takes advantage of a reverse auction where there is one buyer and multiple sellers[33]. While traditional auctions aim to increase bids on an item for sale, reverse auctions strive for the opposite: to drive prices down.

In reverse auctions, the buyer initiates the auction rather than the seller. The buyer identifies a product or service he wants to buy and the starting price which he is willing to pay. Once the auction window is opened, the bidders (e.g. the sellers) compete to offer the products or services at the lowest cost possible while still retaining a profit (see

Figure 5.1). This concept takes advantage of free market competition to lower prices for the buyer.

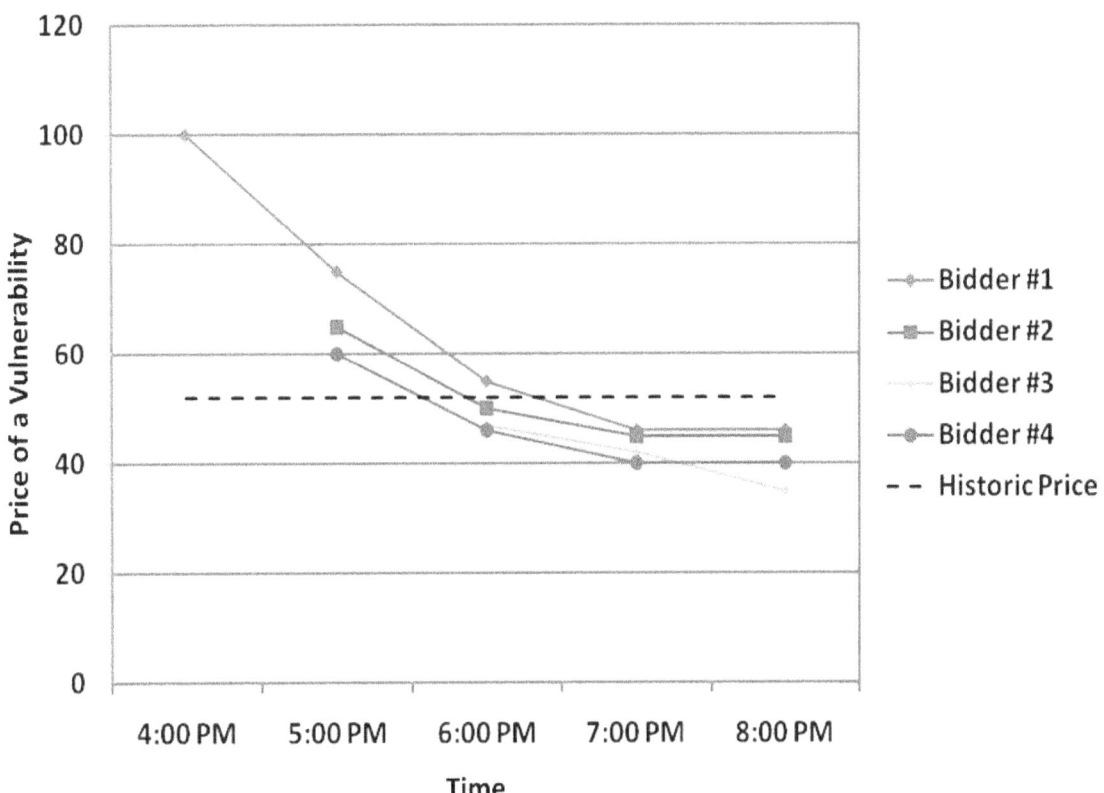

Figure 5.1 Reverse Auction Example: price driven down over time

The purpose of using a reverse auction to discover vulnerabilities is two-fold. The first reason to use a vulnerability auction is to identify possible security issues associated with a software product. By offering cash incentives, vulnerability discovery rates increase based upon the number of researchers attracted to the competition. The greater the number of researchers, the more likely a vulnerability will be found. The second objective is that the vulnerability auction has the potential to provide a meaningful metric which would describe the relative security of a product.

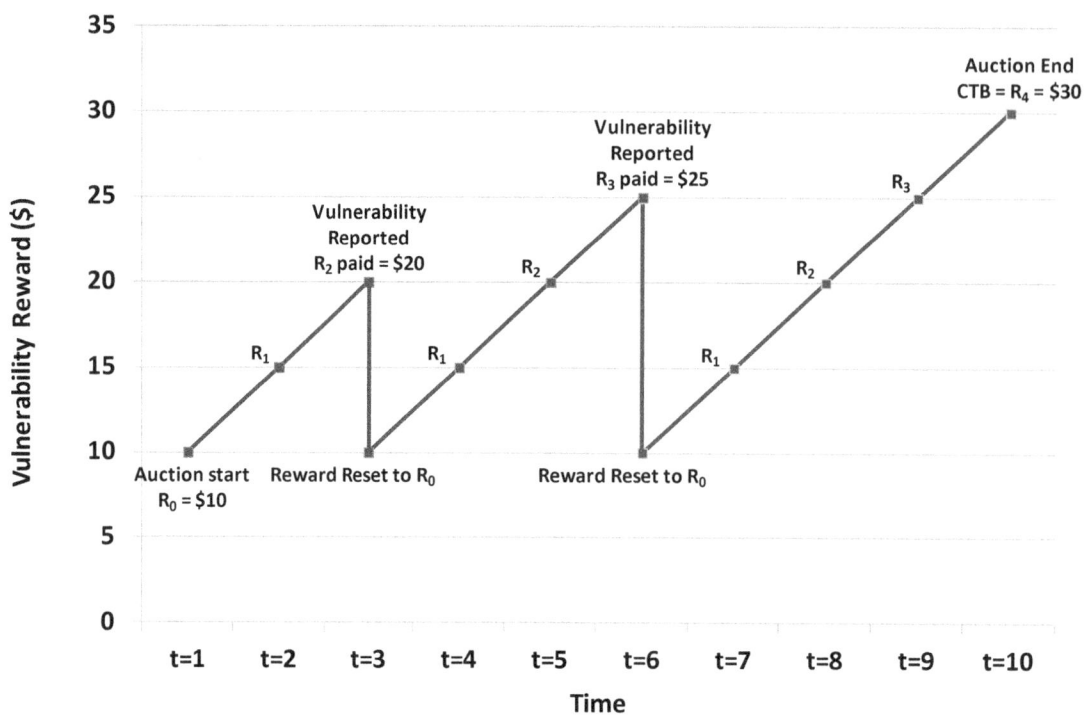

Figure 5.2 Reverse Auction: reward over time

Using a variant of the reverse auction model will allow the government to use auctions for the procurement of software vulnerabilities. The Government (aka. the buyer) would initiate a reverse auction within an identified pool of software researchers (aka. the sellers). The government would identify and provide access to a system they believe to be secure up to R_0 dollars. The objective of the researcher participating in the auction is to disprove the government's assertion. If after a predetermined amount of time a researcher does not report a vulnerability to the government, the reward value increments from R_0 to R_1. In the Figure 5.2 example, the reward first increments from R_0 = \$10 to R_1 = 15\$. This incremental increase repeats until a vulnerability is reported or until the prearranged auction window closes. If a researcher reports a software vulnerability, the government would pay the current value of R_n dollars. The Figure 5.2 example shows vulnerabilities reported at R_2 and R_3 where a researcher is paid \$20 and

44

$25, respectively. At the end of the auction, the last value of the reward, R_4 in the Figure 5.2 example, equates to the security of the system. This final value, the Cost-To-Break (CTB), is the amount of money it costs an individual to discover and report a vulnerability against the information system.

For the DoD vulnerability market to be successful, it is imperative that a substantial set of qualified software researchers participate. As arduous as it is to find and discover software vulnerabilities, the researchers must perceive an adequate level of compensation for their efforts. Compensation to incentivize participation can take many forms in the vulnerability market.

Financial gain is the most common type of incentive offered in the commercial vulnerability market. In March 2012, Forbes Magazine published a vulnerability price list which enumerates the financial value a vulnerability possesses in the open market (reference Table 5.3). The value of these vulnerabilities is a function of a free-market economy and the forces of supply and demand. While the vulnerability may not be worth the cost to the vendor, a potential consumer of vulnerabilities may perceive the cost offsets their risk and any potential costs of using the vulnerability. In any case, if the DoD were to embark on using a vulnerability market and offer cash incentives, it must be cognizant of the value an unreported vulnerability has on the open market.

To establish a financial reward, the DoD must provide additional reassurances in the form of non-attribution and anonymity to the researchers. Non-attribution and anonymity have a value unto themselves. By offering a safe and non-attribution environment, security researchers are welcome to hack a government system without threat of being prosecuted under state and federal law. These reassurances, coupled with a financial

reward, must counter balance the price of a vulnerability on the open market.

Table 5.3 Pricelist for Software Vulnerabilities [13]

Application	Vulnerability Price List
Adobe Reader	$5,000 - $30,000
MAC OSX	$20,000 - $50,000
Android	$30,000 - $60,000
Flash or Java Browser Plug-ins	$40,000 - $100,000
Microsoft Word	$50,000 - $100,000
Windows	$60,000 - $120,000
Firefox or Safari	$60,000 - $150,000
Chrome or Internet Explorer	$80,000 - $200,000
iOS	$100,000 - $250,000

In the free-market economy, a individual's reputation is of significant importance.

Popular e-commerce sites such as Amazon.com and eBay.com have even instituted a

profile field which measures a particular vendor's reputation based upon feedback from

their customers. This is also true in the vulnerability market. In the world of discovering

vulnerabilities, a major motivation among researchers is status. A researcher's status

may be elevated based upon the number of vulnerabilities or new attack vectors

discovered. As hackers in underground forums label their best as "elite," "white-hat"

researchers are also revered in their community. John Arquilla, a professor of defense

analysis at the US Naval Postgraduate School in Monterey, California recently estimated

that there are only around 100 "elite" hackers in the world today [34]. By leveraging the

egos of the limited pool of available researchers, the DoD could incentivize individuals to

participate. A heightened status, while important in underground forums, could also

result in a reputation within industry which leads to job and consulting offers with greater

salaries.

Altruism, in the cyber security environment, is also a powerful motivator. It is so powerful, in fact, that the term "white hat" hacker was developed specifically for the altruistic security movement. The term "white hat" describes a hacker ethically opposed to the abuse of information technology and concerned with improving overall security to benefit society. Traditionally identified as specialists in penetration testing or vulnerability investigation, "white hats" use their expertise to protect computer health and improve system security. After discovering a vulnerability, "white hats" will either contact the vendor directly to force a patch or disclose the vulnerability to a third party like the DHS's NVD.

These incentives, combined with cash rewards resulting from a DoD sponsored vulnerability market, have the propensity to increase software vulnerability discovery rates.

5.4 Cost to Break

As espoused already several times in this paper, complete product security is almost impossible to measure. Metrics, such as, Software Lines of Code can describe complexity of the system but fail to describe overall security. The number of vulnerabilities patched over a given amount of time is also a useful metric that is quantifiable and easily understood. Moreover, a company can advocate the amount of effort (in dollars and time) spent securing a product. The failure of this metric is that a hacker only needs a single undiscovered vulnerability to exploit the system. In order to provide a meaningful way of measuring the security of a system, the DoD requires a metric that is quantifiable, easily understood, dynamic, and supports IT acquisition milestones for decision makers.

The traditional definition of a system's "Cost-to-Break" (CTB) is the cost that an attacker will incur in order to compromise the system. These costs may include money, research time, risk of being caught, etc. Because many of these costs truly vary amongst individuals, calculating this view of the CTB metric is unfeasible. Rather than attempting a CTB metric focused on the individual, this paper proposes using the vulnerability market to evaluate the security of the system by using a large sample population of security researchers.

Using a vulnerability market to calculate the CTB of a system was originally proposed by Dr. Stuart Schechter of Harvard University. In Dr. Schechter's model, the CTB is the result of the market price to discover system defects governed by the presence of competition amongst researchers [6]. Otherwise stated, the market-focused CTB is a product of a vulnerability auction where an IT producer offers a cash prize to free-market researchers to break their system. This strategy of paying researchers to break their systems is actually used frequently today; however, it has yet to be tracked as a true metric. Until 2005, RSA Security Solutions offered an incremental reward for researchers able to break RSA developed encryption keys [35]. Additionally, since 2007 the CanSecWest security conference has hosted the annual Pwn2Own bug challenge which rewards researchers for hacking into some of the most popular computer applications. During the 2013 Pwn2Own challenge, researchers were awarded $480,000 for cracking applications developed by Microsoft, Google, Adobe, Mozilla, and Oracle. Even more impressive, Google claimed theirs was the most secure operating system on the market by offering $110,000 for a browser or system level compromise delivered via a web page. At the end of the conference, the entire Google prize pot of $3.14M remained intact [36].

The inability of researchers attending the conference to crack the application effectively placed the CTB metric for the Google Chrome OS at $110,000. Accordingly, this metric could be used by Google to compare its security to other operating systems (e.g. Windows, Linux). This ability to compare applications is the real value of the CTB metric; the vendor is now able to highlight the security of its product relative to its competitors. For a discerning consumer, the CTB may influence the decision to purchase one product versus another.

The CTB metric may play a role in the DoD, as well. Prior to awarding a contract to a specific vendor, the DoD establishes a source selection[30] strategy or acquisition plan that outlines all evaluation factors and significant sub-factors affecting contract award. Should software security be an evaluation factor in the selection, the CTB would be invaluable in the comparison of multiple vendors. The hope would be that the DoD acquires secure software systems prior to contract award. Additionally, use of the CTB metric could be included in the Joint Capabilities Integration Development System requirement process. By requiring a developed IS meet specified thresholds, the contractor and government will ensure the information system is secure prior to deployment.

5.5 Summary

Although largely conceptual, the application of a vulnerability market within the DoD leads to several beneficial outcomes. First of all, a VM provides an additional

---

[30] Source Selection generally refers to the process of evaluating a competitive bid or proposal to enter into a Government procurement contract.

round of development and operational testing for the government. Secondly, the VM increases information system scrutiny prior to fielding. Increased scrutiny and additional researchers also increases the vulnerability disclosure rate and will result in reducing the total cost of ownership. Thirdly, by the wide use of the VM to enumerate the CTB metric, the government will be able to compare and discern multiple systems.

6. CONCLUSION

"When I initially heard that a company was preparing to offer financial rewards to security bug researchers, my first thought was that it would turn those exploit finders into prostitutes rushing around finding exploits to make a fast buck, but as I thought further on the subject I came to the realization that over the years, everyone had been making money off the work of these researchers except the researchers."
-Marquis Grove, Security News Portal

In this chapter, the conclusions from overall findings are described. Following the conclusions, the recommendations for future research are explained.

6.1 Conclusions

Perfect information security will never be achieved. Whether insecurity is due to the software developer's mistakes, a vendor's unwillingness to fix flaws, or a user unknowingly introducing insecurity, the outcome is the same; valuable information is susceptible to attack. Surprisingly, industry understands the issues of software vulnerability prevalence better than the DoD. In the past decade, dozens of vulnerability markets have sprung into existence based upon the perceived need to enlist non-organic researchers to report application vulnerabilities.

The responsibility for securing data does not lie solely with the vendor or with the product consumer. True information security and management of the risk of unauthorized disclosure is the responsibility of the entire community. While an insecure system increases the risk of cyber attack against the consumer, free market forces will impact the vendor's bottom line.

As demonstrated in Chapter Four, each information system vulnerability has the probabilistic potential to cost the DoD immense resources. Although calculating the consequences of using a system with unknown vulnerabilities is difficult to quantify, discovery of a vulnerability prior to use in an operational environment is more cost effective than remediating it post-deployment. This paper also discussed how to calculate the probabilistic cost of a system's vulnerability. By decomposing the variables in the Single Loss Expectancy equation into it core components (Asset Value, Exposure Factor, and probability of occurrence), the research shows that the greatest impact to security the DoD can have is by lowering the probability of occurrence and by increasing the rate of discovery of system vulnerabilities.

Decreasing the probability and increasing the discovery rate of system vulnerabilities is the primary goal of the proposed vulnerability market model for DoD acquired systems. Not only will the discovery of an unknown vulnerability effectively reduce the probability of a successful attack (using that vulnerability) to 0, lifecycle operations and maintenance costs will also be reduced. Addition of a vulnerability market to the development phase of the acquisition lifecycle will result in a proactive approach to information security and mission assurance.

Lastly, use of the vulnerability auction model proposed in Chapter Five will create a meaningful and easily understandable metric to ensure the DoD acquires systems with security built in. This CTB metric has the propensity to reform the defense industrial base as well as conform to information security requirements as dictated by the warfighter. Through the mutual cooperation between industry and the military in securing information, the DoD will optimize security investments, secure critical information, and provide an effective and resilient warfighting capability.

6.2 Future Research

While the previous section concludes this research project, there remain areas that require additional research in order to truly validate this paper's conclusions. For further research, several suggestions are presented in this section. These suggested areas are not included for a variety of reasons; such as, classification concerns, inability to secure data, and overall scope. The suggestions include:

1. **Use of vulnerability discovery models on DoD information systems**

    As explained in Chapter Four, this analysis assumed an equal likelihood of discovery for each vulnerability. In actuality, every vulnerability does not possess an equal likelihood. This is due to many factors, such as differing complexity within software modules, newly discovered attack vectors, and integration with other components. By using a representative DoD IS vulnerability history, a researcher can advise on the best model to use in predicting vulnerability discovery.

2. **Legality and morality of employing a vulnerability market in the DoD**

    While Appendix B "FAR Policies Relating to Reverse Auctioning" and Appendix C "Legal Considerations" address a few of the legality issues relating to the use of vulnerability markets within the government, much more research is required. Analysis of current national and international law regarding use of such a model is required. Furthermore, is using a government-sponsored VM a moral issue?

3. **In depth cost analysis of cyber attacks against DoD systems**

    In Chapter Four, this paper attempted to define how the quantification of a successful cyber attack could be quantified. In reality, calculating such an impact is beyond the author's ability. Each successful attack has an associated monetary and temporal factor. Further research into this area could provide greater insight on reward values awarded to researchers discovering a system vulnerability.

4. **Impact of composability on information systems**

Finally, this paper did not address the impact of composability on DoD information systems. As it relates to systems engineering, composability deals with the inter-relationships of components. As more components begin interacting with one another, the probability of a system vulnerability grows exponentially. For example, it is possible to connect two seemingly secure systems and the resultant composite system is now insecure.

6.3 Summary

In summation, this paper began by describing the concept of information asymmetry and George Akerlof's Nobel Prize winning work "The Market For Lemons." Stated once more, information asymmetry occurs when the seller knows more about a product than the buyer. As a nation and participants in the global community, the U.S. is responsible for minimizing its consumers' ignorance in every domain; air, land, sea, space, and … cyberspace. The days of trusting a software developer to deliver a completely secure system are over. As soon as the government recognizes and admits that an individual can never be truly secure against the advanced cyber threat, the American public will demand vendor accountability and force a market condition where only the most secure systems survive.

APPENDIX A – DEFINITIONS OF MAC, CL, AND MC

The following definitions are reprinted verbatim from their respective source documents.

Mission Assurance Category
"Applicable to DoD information systems, the mission assurance category reflects the importance of information relative to the achievement of DoD goals and objectives, particularly the warfighters' combat mission. Mission assurance categories are primarily used to determine the requirements for availability and integrity. The Department of Defense has three defined mission assurance categories" (DoDI 8500.2, 2003, Enclosure 2, p. 22).

- **Mission Assurance Category I (MAC I).** "Systems handling information that is determined to be vital to the operational readiness or mission effectiveness of deployed and contingency forces in terms of both content and timeliness. The consequences of loss of integrity or availability of a MAC I system are unacceptable and could include the immediate and sustained loss of mission effectiveness. Mission Assurance Category I systems require the most stringent protection measures" (DoDI 8500.2, 2003, Enclosure 2, p. 22).

- **Mission Assurance Category II (MAC II).** "Systems handling information that is important to the support of deployed and contingency forces. The consequences of loss of integrity are unacceptable. Loss of availability is difficult to deal with and can only be tolerated for a short time. The consequences could include delay or degradation in providing important support services or commodities that may seriously impact mission effectiveness or operational readiness. Mission Assurance Category II systems require additional safeguards beyond best practices to ensure assurance" (DoDI 8500.2, 2003, Enclosure 2, p. 22).

- **Mission Assurance Category III (MAC III).** "Systems handling information that is necessary for the conduct of day-to-day business, but does not materially affect support to deployed or contingency forces in the short-term. The consequences of loss of integrity or availability can be tolerated or overcome without significant impacts on mission effectiveness or operational readiness. The consequences could include the delay or degradation of services or commodities enabling routine activities. Mission Assurance Category III systems require protective measures, techniques, or procedures generally commensurate with commercial best practices" (DoDI 8500.2, 2003, Enclosure 2, pp. 22–23).

Confidentiality Level
"Applicable to DoD information systems, the confidentiality level is primarily used to establish acceptable access factors, such as requirements for individual security clearances or background investigations, access approvals, and need-to-know

determinations; interconnection controls and approvals; and acceptable methods by which users may access the system (e.g., intranet, Internet, wireless). The Department of Defense has three defined confidentiality levels: classified, sensitive, and public" (DoDI 8500.2, 2003, Enclosure 2, p. 16).

Mission Criticality, Mission-Critical Information System
"A system that meets the definitions of 'information system' and 'national security system' in the [Clinger-Cohen Act], the loss of which would cause the stoppage of warfighter operations or direct mission support of warfighter operations. (The designation of mission critical shall be made by a Component Head, a Combatant Commander, or their designee. A financial management IT system shall be considered a mission-critical IT system as defined by the Under Secretary of Defense [Comptroller].) A 'Mission-Critical Information Technology System' has the same meaning as a 'Mission-Critical Information System'" (DoDI 5000.02, p. 48, Table 8).

Mission-Essential Information System
"A system that meets the definition of 'information system' in Reference (v), that the acquiring Component Head or designee determines is basic and necessary for the accomplishment of the organizational mission. (The designation of mission-essential shall be made by a Component Head, a Combatant Commander, or their designee. A financial management IT system shall be considered a mission-essential IT system as defined by the [Under Secretary of Defense (Comptroller)].) A 'Mission-Essential Information Technology System' has the same meaning as a 'Mission- Essential Information System'" (DoDI 5000.02, 2008, Table 8, p. 48.).

Mission-Support Information System
If the information system is neither mission-critical nor mission-essential, it is labeled mission support (based on DoDI 8510.01, 2007, p. 37, Table E3.A1.T1).

APPENDIX B – FAR POLICIES RELATING TO REVERSE AUCTIONING

FAR Part 1.102 (d)

Permissible exercise of authority (FAR Part 1.102 (d)) - states that government procurement personnel may assume a specific strategy, practice, policy or procedure is in the best interests of the Government and is not addressed in the FAR, nor prohibited by law (statute or case law), Executive order or other regulation, that the strategy, practice, policy or procedure is a permissible exercise of authority.

FAR Part 4.5

Use of Electronic Commerce (FAR Part 4.5) - states that "The Federal Government shall use electronic commerce whenever practical or cost-effective."

FAR Part 14.202-8

Electronic bids (FAR 14.202-8) - This section allows the use of electronic commerce for submission of bids and FAR 14.303 allows bids to be modified or withdrawn by any means authorized in the solicitation.

FAR Part 15.002

Competitive acquisitions (FAR Part 15.002) - The FAR states that "when contracting in a competitive environment, the procedures of this part are intended to minimize the complexity of the solicitation, the evaluation, and the source selection decision, while maintaining a process designed to foster an impartial and comprehensive evaluation of offerors' proposals, leading to selection of the proposal representing the best value to the Government."

FAR Part 15.306 (e)(3))

Limits on Exchanges (FAR 15.306(e)(3)) states that Government personnel involved in the acquisition shall not engage in conduct that reveals an offeror's price without that offeror's permission. However, the contracting officer may inform an offeror that its price is considered by the Government to be too high or too low, and reveal the results of the analysis supporting that conclusion. It is also permissible, at the Government's discretion, to indicate to all offerors the cost or price that the Government's price analysis, market research, and other reviews have identified as reasonable (41 U.S.C. 423(h)(1)(2).

APPENDIX C – LEGAL CONSIDERATIONS

Digital Millennium Copyright Act

The Digital Millennium Copyright Act, or DMCA, was signed into law on October 28, 1998 by President Bill Clinton. Under the DMCA, it is now a criminal act to "circumvent technological measures used by copyright owners to protect their works" and to tamper "with copyright management information" [37]. The DMCA also includes criminal penalties for violating the prohibitions. The DMCA's primary purpose is to protect the intellectual property (IP) of those individuals or companies that produce digital information. As the DoD acquisition process rarely ever purchases the intellectual rights to the information technology it purchases (because of the cost), this act encumbers a government's authoritative decision to pursue a vulnerability auction. For the DoD to require a defense contractor to release their intellectual property (e.g. source-code, system configuration, encryption algorithms) to a group of uncleared researchers, the government must pay for the IP rights. This provision of the contract may be cost-prohibitive based on the size and complexity of the system.

Uniform Trade Secrets Act

The Uniform Trade Secrets Act, or UTSA, was initially published in 1979 and amended in 1985. The UTSA seeks to standardize protection of industry trade secrets at the U.S. state level by defining the rights companies have in protecting their IP. The UTSA defines a trade secret as "information, including a formula, pattern, compilation, program, device, method, technique, or process, that: (i) derives independent economic value, actual or potential, from not being generally known to, and not being readily ascertainable by proper means by, other persons who can obtain economic value from its disclosure or use, and (ii) is the subject of efforts that are reasonable under the circumstances to maintain its secrecy." Moreover, theft of a trade secret is defined as the "intent to convert a trade secret that is related to or included in a product … to the economic benefit of anyone other than the owner thereof, and intending or knowing that the offense will, injure any owner of that trade secret."

If the DoD conducts a vulnerability auction with a company's closed source code and a researcher discovers a system vulnerability, the company may sue the government and the individual if he/she chooses to disclose the vulnerability. The company may choose litigation for a couple of reasons. If the fix to the vulnerability is cost prohibitive, the company may choose not to remediate it. Also, if disclosing the vulnerability causes negative economic impact (e.g. stock valuation, company reputation) the producer may not want the vulnerability disclosed. If either of the two cases is present, the company would seek restitution under the UTSA.

Homeland Security Act

Section 1016(e) of the 2001 PATRIOT Act explicitly protects "critical infrastructure," a term that includes "systems and assets, whether physical or virtual, so vital to the United States that the incapacity or destruction of such systems and assets would have a debilitating impact on security, national economic security, national public health or safety, or any combination of those matters."

APPENDIX D – DOD VM CONCEPT OF OPERATIONS

Base Assumptions

To establish the reward and increment schedule, the government needs to make the following market assumptions:

1. All participants are rational actors and have full and equal access to the test environment.
2. This assumption is critical as no rational security researcher will undertake the challenge of finding a system vulnerability if the average reward (Rn) of submitting a vulnerability report exceeds the average cost of finding a vulnerability.
3. Multiple researchers participate in the auction and no researcher knows each other's cost of discovering a vulnerability.

As the tools for exploiting known vulnerabilities (e.g. Metasploit) are easily accessible and widely used, the "low hanging fruit" will be reported early in the auction. It is incumbent upon the government to ensure all known defects are patched to the system prior to test environment development.

Test Planning

The first step in setting up a VM auction is to determine what information will be released by the government in order for researchers to test the system in question. Information may take many forms, such as, application and network architecture, data-flow diagrams, use cases, application source code, compiled executables, and application programming interfaces to name a few. Special consideration should be made to determining the amount and detail of information to provide to the auction. In cases of applications used to optimize the confidentiality of the data it stores/manipulates, a less detailed suite of information can be provided. Compromise of system information can also be limited based upon the clearance of the researchers chosen to partake in the VM.

Once the information to be distributed is finalized, the test environment should be defined as accurately as possible. The test environment can be distributed virtually through the application of a virtual machine or centralized in a specific location. This test environment, virtually distributed or centrally located, must be maintained under strict configuration management (CM) and separated from any development environment. Strict CM will ensure that the environment can periodically be refreshed to ensure no intentional or inadvertent modification of the system under test.

Reward Increment and Schedule

Once the test plan is formulated and prior to executing the vulnerability auction, the government should publish the reward increment schedule, R(t), where R is the reward amount at time t.

The reward increment is dependent on the application being tested. In order to determine the initial offering, R0, several factors are under consideration. Factors to consider include the value of the system being tested (including the value of the information), potential application exposure to the government, complexity (SLOC), tools required to test, and number of potential researchers. Also, R0 should be chosen carefully. A low R0 could reduce the cost of the auction but fail to attract a sufficient volume of security researchers. An R0 too high allows little room to increment rewards in a fiscally constrained test budget.

Once R0 is established, the reward increment, $R(t+1)$, and increment timing, t, needs to be established. Referencing assumption #3 above, the "low hanging fruit" will quickly be reported and subsequently reset $R(t)$ to R0. As vulnerabilities begin to require more complex analysis, the time between reported vulnerabilities will increase. In order to entice the researchers to report the more complex vulnerabilities, the reward must increment upwards as an incentive to detect and report. As with setting the value of R0, incremental increases to the reward must also be carefully considered. An incremental increase too small will discourage the researchers from investing additional analysis into finding vulnerabilities. An incremental increase too large will quickly reach the upper budgetary limit.

The rate of incremental reward increases also serves to encourage vulnerability reporting. Referencing assumption #2, no researcher knows the cost for another researcher to find a vulnerability. Should a researcher discover a vulnerability and wait to disclose it to the trusted third party for validation, another researcher could claim the reward while the other is waiting. The consequence of waiting would be an automatic reset of $R(t)$ to R0.

List of Eligible and Verified Researchers

In the circumstance where the government chooses to limit the pool of researchers based upon the sensitivity related to system specification disclosure, certain participation requirements should be enforced. For example, a requirement may be levied to exclude those researchers with affiliation to foreign governments, those without a certain level of clearance, or those with evidence of unlawful activity. The pool of researchers meeting the auction requirements will be verified by the trusted third party prior to the auction information disclosure.

In order to maximize the full benefit of a vulnerability auction, the government should seek to limit the barriers to participation. The higher the participation, the more likely that undiscovered vulnerabilities will be reported.

Trusted Third Party

A Trusted Third Party (TTP) is a commonly used intermediary for network security. In network security and cryptography, a TTP is an entity where two or more parties "trust" the TTP to facilitate communications. The most common use of a TTP is in the practice of acting as a certificate authority in email exchange or webpage access. The certificate authority (e.g. Verisign, GoDaddy, and Comodo) issues digital certificates to individuals, organizations, and websites in order for other individuals to verify the content as trusted.

In the vulnerability market, the TTP's job is to assess a researcher's submitted vulnerability report for uniqueness, potential impact to the information system, and validity. The TTP also ensures researcher anonymity (if requested) be maintained and timely payments are made for a valid report. Moreover, the TTP would manage the market based upon the government's stipulations of timeline, incremental reward increases, and eligible participants.

VM Execution

Once the test plan and environment are developed, reward increment and scheduled are determined, list of eligible participants is collated, and TTP assigned the VM can be executed and monitored.

BIBLIOGRAPHY

[1]   Akerlof, George A. "The market for" lemons": Quality uncertainty and the market mechanism." The quarterly journal of economics (1970): 488-500.

[2]   Camp, L. Jean, Economics of Information Security (January 2006).

[3]   "Measuring the Cost of Cybercrime," by Ross Anderson, University of Cambridge; Chris Barton, Cloudmark; Rainer Böhme, University of Münster; Richard Clayton, University of Cambridge; Michel J.G. van Eeten, Delft University of Technology; Michael Levi, Cardiff University; Tyler Moore, Southern Methodist University; and Stefan Savage, University of California, San Diego.

[4]   Rainer Böhme, "Vulnerability Markets: What Is the Economic Value of a Zero-Day Exploit?" Proceedings of 22C3, Berlin, Germany, December 27-30, 2005.

[5]   Anderson, Ross. "Why Information Security is Hard – An economic perspective". Computer Security Applications Conference, 2001. ACSAC 2001.

[6]   Schechter, Stuart. How to buy better testing: Using competition to get the most security and robustness for your dollar. In Infrastructure Security Conference, October 2002. Bristol, UK.

[7]   Department of Defense. (2006, July 7). Defense acquisition guidebook (Ver. 1.6). Retrieved October 30, 2012, from http://akss.dau.mil/dag.

[8]   Marchenko, Artem, and Pekka Abrahamsson, "Predicting Software Defect Density: A Case Study on Automated Static Code Analysis," Agile Processes in Software Engineering and Extreme Programming, Berlin: Springer, 2007.

[9]   Defense Science Board Task Force, "Department of Defense Policies and Procedures for the Acquisition of Information Technology." March, 2009, http://www.acq.osd.mil/dsb/reports/ADA498375.pdf (Accessed October 26, 2012).

[10] "US-CERT - United States Computer Emergency Readiness Team." US-CERT - United States Computer Emergency Readiness Team. N.p., n.d. http://www.us-cert.gov/ (Accessed September 6, 2012).

[11] HP Enterprise Security, "Zero Day Initiative (ZDI)." http://www.hpenterprisesecurity.com/products/hp-dvlabs/zero-day-initiative-zdi (Accessed September 12, 2012).

[12] Desautels, Adriel. "Selling Zero-day's Doesn't Increase Your Risk, Here's Why. | Netragard's SNOsoft Research Team." N.p., 8 Aug. 2012. Web. http://pentest.netragard.com/2012/08/13/selling-zero-days-doesnt-increase-your-risk-heres-why/ (Accessed October 5, 2012).

[13] Greenberg, Andy. (2012, March 23). Shopping For Zero-Days: A Price List For Hackers' Secret Software Exploits. http://www.forbes.com/sites/andygreenberg/2012/03/23/shopping-for-zero-days-an-price-list-for-hackers-secret-software-exploits/ (Accessed September 12, 2012).

[14] Hofmann, Marcia, "Zero-day Exploit Sales Should Be Key Point in Cybersecurity Debate." March 12, 2012, https://www.eff.org/deeplinks/2012/03/zero-day-exploit-sales-should-be-key-point-cybersecurity-debate (Accessed September 5, 2012).

[15] SecurityFocus, "SecurityFocus." N.p., n.d. Web. http://www.securityfocus.com/ (Accessed September 5, 2012).

[16] Wilson, Clay. "Computer Attack and Cyber Terrorism: Vulnerabilities and Policy Issues for Congress." CRS Report for Congress. October 17, 2003.

[17] United States. Department of Defense. USD. DoD Information Security Program. N.p., 24 Febuary 2012. http://www.dtic.mil/whs/directives/corres/pdf/520001_vol1.pdf (Accessed September 5, 2012).

[18] DODD 8500.1 Information Assurance, October 24, 2002.

[19] U.S. Department of Defense Directive 8500.01E, "Information Assurance," current as of April 23, 2007.

[20] Chairman of the Joint Chiefs of Staff Instruction 6510.01, "Information Assurance and Support to Computer Network Defense," February 9, 2011.

[21] National Security Presidential Directive – 54 / Homeland Security Presidential Directive 23 (NSPD-54/ HSPD-23). January 2008.

[22] Detica and Office of Cyber Security and Information Assurance. The cost of cyber crime, February 2011. http://www.cabinetoffice.gov.uk/resource-library/cost-of-cyber-crime.

[23] Younis, Awad A., H. Joh, and Y. K. Malaiya, "Modeling Learningless Vulnerability Discovery using a Folded Distribution," sam'11, The 2011 International Conference on Security and Management. 2011.

[24] Federal Acquisition Regulation. https://www.aqusisition.gov/far/html (Accessed September 12, 2012).

[25] Linister, Bruce g.. "Auctions in Defense Acquisition: Theory and Experimental Evidence." Acquisition review quarterly , no. Summer 2002 (2002).

[26] Schwalb, Micah. "Exploit Derivitives & National Security". Yale Journal of Law and Technology. Vol 9. January 2007.

[27] Craver, Scott, "Reading between the lines: Lessons from the SDMI challenge." August 17, 2001, http://static.usenix.org/events/sec01/craver.pdf (Accessed September 12, 2012).

[28] Mozilla foundation, "Mozilla foundation announces security bug bounty program." August 2, 2004, http://www.mozilla.org/press/mozilla-2004-08-02.html (Accessed September 5, 2012).

[29] Microsoft, "Microsoft Announces Anti-Virus Reward Program." November 5, 2003, http://www.microsoft.com/presspass/press/2003/nov03/11-05AntiVirusRewardsPR.mspx (Accessed September 5, 2012).

[30] Lemos, Robert, "Ebay pulls excel vulnerability auction." December 10, 2005., http://www.theregister.co.uk/2005/12/10/ebay_pulls_excel_vulnerability_auction/ (Accessed September 05, 2012.).

[31] Naraine, Ryan, "eBay Pulls Bidding for MS Excel Vulnerability." December 09, 2005, http://www.eweek.com/c/a/Security/eBay-Pulls-Bidding-for-MS-Excel-Vulnerability/ (Accessed September 5, 2012).

[32] Defense Acquisition University. "Fundamentals of Reverse Auctioning". https://DAU.mil (Accessed September 12, 2012).

[33] Ozment, Andy. "Bug auctions: Vulnerability markets reconsidered." In Third Workshop on the Economics of Information Security. 2004.

[34] Carroll, Rory. "US urged to recruit master hackers to wage cyber war on America's foes." The Guardian. 10 July 2012. Web. http://www.guardian.co.uk/technology/2012/jul/10/us-master-hackers-al-qaida (Accessed December 6, 2012).

[35] http://www.rsasecurity.com/rsalabs/challenges/factoring.numbers.html (dated 31 December 2005)(Accessed March 13, 2013).

[36] Thomson, I. "Pwn2Own: IE10, Firefox, Chrome, Reader, Java hacks land $500k." http://www.theregister.co.uk/2013/03/08/pwn2own_contest_cansecwest/ (Accessed March 13, 2013).

[37] U. S. Copyright service, "The Digital Millenium Copyright Act." December, 1998, http://www.copyright.gov/legislation/dmca.pdf (Accessed September 12, 2012).

[38] U.S. Department of Defense Instruction 5000.02, "Operation of the Defense Acquisition System," December 8, 2008.

[39] U.S. Department of Defense Instruction 8510.01, "DoD Information Assurance Certification and Accreditation Process (DIACAP)," November 28, 2007.

[40] A. A. Younis, H. Joh, and Y. K. Malaiya, "Modeling Learningless Vulnerability Discovery using a Folded Distribution," sam'11, The 2011 International Conference on Security and Management, pp. 617-623, 2011.